Crank 'em Up!!!

Crank 'em Up!!!

Brilliant sales contests and bright ideas to turn on your team and turn up results

Bruce Fuller

Self-Counsel Press
a division of
International Self-Counsel Press Ltd.
Canada   U.S.A.

Printed in Canada

First edition: January, 1995; Reprinted: April, 1995

Canadian Cataloguing in Publication Data
    Fuller, Bruce, 1942-
    Crank 'em up

    (Self-counsel business series)
    ISBN 0-88908-799-7
    1. Sales management.   2. Selling — Competitions.
I. Title.   II. Series.
HF5438.4.F84   1994   658.8'1   C94-910927-4

Cover photography by Andy Stokes, ATN Visuals, Vancouver, B.C.
Cartoons by Bruce Fuller © 1994.

Self-Counsel Press
a division of
International Self-Counsel Press Ltd.

Head and Editorial Office	*U.S. Address*
1481 Charlotte Road	1704 N. State Street
North Vancouver, British Columbia	Bellingham, Washington
Canada V7J 1H1	98225

To Todd, Chantal, and Nadine, of the first batch, and to Lauren, of the second batch. To Karen, for your prodding along the way, for your partnership at Pacific Partners, and for doing more with less in tight times. Oh yes, and for leaving the Mac memory untouched of your tennis notes.

Contents

ix

Part 2
Brilliant Sales Contests

Checklists

Worksheets

Samples

Acknowledgments

Most of my appreciation has to go out to those hundreds of salespeople who embraced some pretty crazy contest schemes over the years and who enthusiastically spun the themes into their day-to-day selling with both Neon Products and Claude Neon, two sister operating entities of the world's largest sign company at The Jim Pattison Group.

Thanks to Jimmy Pattison for his friendly tutelage and sage "business: just gotta be fun!" advice that I still have no problem buying into.

And thanks to all those management executives with whom I enjoyed brainstorming and who believed that promoting sales and achieving end-of-month quota figures meant more than cramming a briefcase with blank orders and expecting customers to sign them; that approaching business development recipes with a healthy dollop of creativity could really make the difference. Their patience allowed me to take whatever time I needed to wander the aisles of downtown toy stores where I got a lot of my ideas from. They listened to me expound at great length about what this little windup airplane, or that battery-operated army tank, or those toy soldiers could do when it came to crunching through with hard sales orders for our factories.

I'm thankful for productive hours of conceptualizing with mentors Stan Whittle, Bob Oliphant, and Ron Errett.

Thanks also go to a solid gang of field sales managers who had to carry the spirit and energy of promotional launches through their everyday department management. (Try that in white-out blizzard conditions at -40°, huh Wynn?)

For all those folks behind the scenes in offices across the country: brilliant design teams, manufacturing specialists, installers, and service crews...your participation and supportive enthusiasm helped create the very best selling environment that troops could wish for.

And my gratitude to Bob Sinclair: sometimes associate, sometimes client, sometimes supplier, and at all times that solid friend and sturdy backboard for the bouncing of a myriad of creative concepts... and who has only stolen a few.

And now, well over a dozen years since those wacky times, thanks to some special clients who paid my Pacific Partners well (but never quite enough!) for creative strategies, marketing directions, sales promotional concepts, contest ideas, and a slew of communications devices that apparently worked where it all counted — at their cash registers.

And to Self-Counsel Press President, Diana Douglas, and Director of Marketing, Pat Touchie: thanks for that encouragement when you first visited my office and saw the neat contest toys and theme stuff. To your Managing Editor and author-coach, Ruth Wilson: with your kind of stick-handling, you could've played center for Team Canada.

To the team members of the 1986 Everest Light Expedition who, in my mind, *all* reached the summit of that big momma mountain and taught me the correct spelling of ATTITUDE.

Introduction

This is a book about those special natural "highs" you get when you sell something. And it's about how to multiply those highs by making sales happen in a bigger way through organizing and running sales contests. And to me, contesting is great fun.

"Business: just gotta be fun!" said Jimmy Pattison, the self-made multimillionaire owner of The Jim Pattison Group of Vancouver, British Columbia, and my former boss. He told me time and time again, "Bruce, when you stop having fun at doing business, then you'd better move along to something else."

So this book is about having fun and doing business, finding and getting deals, and closing orders and moving goods in slack times, tough times, no-budget times, recessionary times, and often against those all-too-familiar, much lower-priced competitors who get in the way by giving it away.

In 1969, when I joined the Neon Products organization as the company's national marketing co-ordinator, one of my first introductions to the firm was an involvement in the structuring of the annual sales contest which made the business of selling even more fun. It was absolutely amazing the deals that we closed when our salespeople and customers were having a good time. Yes, the customers, too, often got to play in our contests.

As my marketing career matured through the responsibilities of field sales management, branch management, regional and divisional sales management, vice president sales, then vice president marketing, I was fortunate to have free rein to conceptualize, design, write, launch, execute, monitor, and help celebrate the success of all our national sales contests with bang-up conferences.

This good fortune was further extended because I worked with a willing and cooperative management group who gave me plenty of rope and genuine encouragement to experiment with the zaniest of schemes. Not only were those people completely supportive of the plans I proposed, but they also approved the all-important budgets necessary to seed the developmental stages of what were, for the most part, unproven ideas. Generally speaking, they were an executive team quite secure in their own managerial abilities, believing in themselves and in me, and not having to cover their collective backsides with wavering indecision.

I mention this because if you're a sales manager who spends half your time butting heads with the rest of the management team, always plodding uphill with your ideas, I'm afraid you'll never really appreciate what true success is all about. I suppose it's traditional in most companies to hear sarcastic comments like, "There goes Sales spending all our money," "How come Sales gets to go on those neat trips?" and "Are contests *necessary*?" If it gets you down, then you must consider where you want to be in the organization.

One way to handle this is to get everyone on-side for contest time. I don't believe that contests are only for sales people. Whenever possible, budget the whole organization into the plan. Involve absolutely everyone. And by involving departmental management in other areas of the company (production, finance, accounting, administration, distribution, service, etc.), and finding innovative ways to tie them into the final sales numbers you are budgeting for, you'll be amazed at how turned-on and suddenly supportive your colleagues will become.

The management group I worked with also allowed me the sort of flexibility in their budgeting to include provisions for sales management's continuing professional education. In addition to their support in the unique and specialist areas of sales contesting, they allowed me plenty of leeway when it came to educating myself and my team of sales managers. Thus, we were able to source out the best sales and marketing management educational programs and resource materials available in Canada and the United States, and in this book I draw on much of what we learned during that time.

You, too, need to learn everything you can. Sales management and sales contesting doesn't just happen; you must develop a distinct understanding of what motivates, satisfies, and cranks up a sales force in order to set strategies and develop plans that jump-start sales. I recommend that you establish a tight little cross-indexed library of background research data and training tools as you pick up new ideas and use the contest themes and ideas in this book.

Without question some of the most reliable, best-presented, understandable, and totally usable information comes from the Chicago-based Dartnell Corporation. Their materials come packaged in hardcover, academic-style volumes or extremely user-friendly three-ring binders. Dartnell's *How to Conduct Successful Sales Contests and Incentive Programs* by David Seltz was the bible I referred to most often. Using the basic background information and case studies presented as contest staples for my recipe, I stirred into the promotional stew pot plenty of creativity and concept graphics fine-tuned by select artists recruited from our 60-member, award-winning design department.

Throughout *Crank 'Em Up!!!*, you'll spot plenty of references to points picked up in this and various other Dartnell publications that have been so important to my marketing management career. I certainly suggest that your business library will never be complete without their presence on the shelves.

What follows in this book is also drawn on my more recent experience running my own company. Following some 14 years of stick-handling four to six national sales contests a year plus numerous "instant" promotions with both Neon Products and Claude Neon, then a change of responsibilities to wind up at our head office as The Jim Pattison Group's corporate affairs vice president, I found myself mired in a dilemma. It just wasn't the blast it used to be — no fun anymore — so at that point I left the relative security of a pension plan behind and founded a small marketing communications company, Pacific Partners Communications Group, that has grown quite respectably since its inception.

A key phrase in our mission statement when establishing Pacific Partners was *to have fun doing business.* So for the most part, I'm back to terrific days again. Virtually every client we've worked with has provided a fertile flower bed for our creative seedlings and a wonderful climate for their nurturing, growth, and blossoming.

Clients give me ample opportunities to stick my hand into the furthest corners of the contest and promotional bag of tricks and pull winners for them. Sure, they raise an eyebrow now and then, but for the most part all have been wonderful in running along with me.

It's my sincere hope that this book will be fun for you to read, and along with the smiles, you'll pick up an idea or two that cranks up your sales force and helps you along the road to strong business success in your own sales management career. If you would like to share some of your experiences with me, or if you want me to critique one of your own sales contests, see the back of the book for where to contact me.

You'll find the book sprinkled with tidbits and gems I've picked up from some of the best in the sales and marketing management business. And since I've always enjoyed illustrating my thoughts on the flip chart at sales meetings, I've also dropped a few doodles into the pages ahead.

Now let's address your sales targets and your sales people whose job it is to hit the budget bull's-eye. **Let's crank 'em up!!!**

Part 1

Managing Your Team: Elements of Successful Sales Management

1

Taking Stock:
You as the Sales Manager

Before you even start to read through this book, I think you owe it to yourself to take a few minutes off. Sit back at your desk, loosen any constricting garments that might be clawing at your jugular (like too-tight ties or fancy scarfs, those noose-type management things), allow some fresh air to penetrate the inner sanctum of your sales office, and have a serious little heart-to-heart with yourself. Ask yourself: *Deep down in my quota-hardened guts, am I up for it? Do I really want to be in the sales management game?*

It makes absolutely no sense to have a sales-related title on your business card unless you're prepared to genuinely commit, and then buy into, what selling is all about. You have to make that purchase from the most honest recesses of your deal-making heart.

No one's listening in right now and you're accountable only to yourself. It's time to be brutally honest. Why did you pick up this book? Is it because you feel passionately that you're really in the right slot? Or is it because you're not up to it and you're looking for a "quick fix?"

Forget what your family, friends, and colleagues would say if you went back to the sales force. Forget that it's a bit of an ego trip to lord it over a collection of souls whose lot in life

3

will always be to toil over the phones, methodically grinding through their search for a treasure trove of new leads or mother lode of hot prospects with out-of-the-way addresses and hard-to-find parking spots. Oh, and yes, if you had to go to your high school reunion next week, forget about your image suffering if you told all those old classmates, "I'm a sales rep."

Do you love the sales management challenge enough to toss your car keys back on the desk at 4:30 in the afternoon, call off the tennis match, and stick around until who-knows-when because it gives you a helluva lot of satisfaction to come up with a great new idea for tomorrow's first sales meeting of the month? Because setting up tomorrow's sales meeting gets all your creative juices going and you really can't wait until the door closes behind the last rep in so you can get them cranked?

If you really do feel that way, then you'll probably get excited by the ideas and contest themes presented in this book. But sales management is not for everyone.

Yes, it's tremendously important for sales managers to have developed selling skills, to know the product, to know the market, and to understand the required techniques of prospecting, uncovering leads and needs, presenting, negotiating, closing, and servicing. But sales managers also need a few other skills like motivating, coaching, teaching, creating an environment that encourages rather than discourages — those skills that make the job of selling into the career of deal making.

Managing a national sales force of, for example, 3,500 salespeople operating through 26 regional offices and their 150 branches, and selling 206 products to 50,000 key accounts is not necessarily the right fit for today's just-announced salesperson-of-the-week.

This is even more obvious in smaller sales department operations. It's very easy to spot the boss's favorite when the department is bulging at the seams with six salespeople, but can this month's winner build a sales department that will one day see the sales force expand into many regional locations with a multimillion-dollar sales revenue budget?

We all know very well that a company's best salesperson can become a worst nightmare sales manager. Is this you? Are you a result of the infamous "Peter Principle," that people rise to the level of their incompetence?

Are you happy in the sales manager role? Do you grin at yourself in the rearview mirror on the way to sales meetings? And does that face still grin back on the way home?

Do you have the right attitude? Today it really doesn't matter if you're managing just a handful of people representing your company or if you've got a national challenge; if your attitude isn't quite where it should be, you might want to consider a move.

It's difficult to gauge your own attitude unless you're prepared to take a close, honest look in the mirror. Use the short quiz in Worksheet #1 to help you assess your attitudes in an objective way.

Worksheet #1
The Sales Manager's Attitude Quiz

Answer each question with a score of 1 to 5, based on what best reflects your attitude and management style at this time in your career.

1 = Disagree.	"I hate this area; it's the last damn thing I want to think about!"
2 = Sort of agree.	"Okay, I know I've got to get at it, so I'll struggle through."
3 = Agree most of the time.	"Yes, I'm into this; it's important to my sales objectives."
4 = Agree.	"High on my list of sales management priorities."
5 = Agree strongly.	"Wow, this area turns my crank. Love it!"

1. I understand what motivates my people to sell. ＿＿＿

2. Sales offices should be happy environments. ＿＿＿

3. Salespeople should participate in decision making. ＿＿＿

4. Selling has to be fun for everyone. ＿＿＿

5. Salespeople have to "buy into" their sales quotas. ＿＿＿

6. I'm *personally* interested in my sales reps' job needs. ＿＿＿

7. In a dispute, I go to the line for my salespeople. ＿＿＿

8. I understand strategic planning. ____

9. This company is nothing without sales. ____

10. My knowledge of our products/services is excellent. ____

11. I've got enough education to do this job right. ____

12. I'll go to bat for my people any time. ____

13. I'm happy to see others out there doing the selling. ____

14. Sales training works. ____

15. Sales contesting is important for hitting sales objectives. ____

16. I'm really into coaching. ____

17. I promote team play. ____

18. Using a big stick doesn't get results. ____

19. Even the best reps should follow policy. ____

20. My salespeople get the benefit of the doubt. ____

The interesting thing about this quiz is that it got you thinking, didn't it? You can't fail the exercise. It's purpose wasn't to get you packing your briefcase, but to get your mind into some of the areas I feel a sales manager's mind should be. Go back to each question one more time and revisit the scores you assigned. If everything in the questionnaire bothers you to the point where you're wondering about your slot in the company hierarchy, then maybe you do have to rethink your career choice and leave this little book in the top drawer of your desk for the next person in your chair.

But since 99.99% of those who read this will feel challenged to move positively forward, we had better take a quick look at one of the more elementary steps in creating a sales force: the challenge of hiring.

2

Best-Bet, Gut-Feel Hiring

I'm a believer in name brands — products that have weathered the test of time and have boldly elbowed their way into my life both at home and at the office. When I was Vice President Marketing for The Jim Pattison Group, I investigated dozens of name-brand, well-known, proven, field-tested, and affordable training programs available for sales management. Most of them offered good advice for proper hiring techniques and provided plenty of paperwork exercises, ideal forms, and tricky tests that eager-to-hire managers could copy and use back at their offices. And while our organization used a number of them successfully, when the hiring exercise got right down to the final choices, I'd always tell a sales manager, "Hire by that inner voice...use your guts. Remember that *your* success is entirely dependent on the success of those you hire!"

So despite my faith in proven hiring programs and techniques, I also believe in the *gut-feel* method. I should warn you that I don't jump right into the gut-feel approach without considering a few other things like experience, resumes, and background checks. And I sometimes run a test or two. But those first few minutes with a candidate are the most important to my decision making. I believe this is especially important in sales because your new salesperson will be spending a lot of "first few minutes" with new clients who are trying to decide whether to spend their money on you, your product, or your service.

a. The Not-So-Sophisticated Hiring Test

For me, hiring is a lot like buying a tie. I shop around a bit and see what I feel most comfortable with. If the color (personality, sense of humor, and attitude) fits with where I'm coming from, then I get right down to the decision making. I rarely use the scientific approach of laying the tie beside a number of suit patterns, shirts, etc. I just say, "This one will work. How much?"

I realize, of course, that hiring is different because you're dealing with human beings. The hiring decision has to be a little more thorough than the one to buy a tie, which you can wear for a couple of days and then leave on the rack until the next garage sale. It's not so simple dealing with human beings in the job market, and these days it's getting progressively more difficult to "de-hire" if you do decide you've made a mistake.

When you're in the hiring mode, don't forget good hiring practices, the law, labor codes, legal rights of the individual, and, again, the fact that it's easy to hire and tougher to fire!

When you are hiring, you can use Worksheet #2 to help with your decision making. You should depend a lot on your candid, off-the-cuff responses to the questions in this worksheet. No one needs to listen to your answers, so you can say anything you want.

Worksheet #2
The Not-So-Sophisticated Hiring Test

Use the questions in this worksheet for each candidate you interview. Score each of the questions on a scale of 1 to 10. Someone who scores close to 100 points is a better bet than someone who scrapes by with a 51.

____ 1. If I owned this company, and it was my own money, would I honestly hire this person?

____ 2. If I were a prospective customer of this outfit, would I like to do business with this person?

____ 3. Does this person listen?

____ 4. Does this person know anything about my company? Has he or she researched us? Know what we do? How we do it?

____ 5. Does this person understand what my needs as a sales manager are?

____ 6. Eyeball to eyeball, do I feel I could trust this person?

____ 7. If I moved up the ladder, could this person set an example for the rest of the salespeople?

____ 8. If I introduced a sales contest in the next few weeks, would this person be in the top five?

____ 9. Would I feel okay about introducing this person to our best account and letting him or her handle the business? Once he or she learns and knows our products?

____ 10. Attitude: out of a possible best score of 10, does this person score more than 8?

While everything you learn about your candidate will help you make a decision, always remember that no one is perfect. You'll find flaws and skeletons in the best of closets. You've probably had your share of money problems, divorce problems, kids' problems, tax problems, health problems, customer problems, and boss problems. I know I have. When I'm hiring, I think back to the times I sat on the other side of the desk and had as much baggage to conceal as anyone.

If possible, I like to get to know a little about the candidate's partner on the home front. While this is important no matter where a salesperson is located, I've found that in the smaller, more remote regional offices where there are fewer people to communicate with, the support a person gets on the home front has a lot to do with success. Also, it's another route to understanding where the candidate is coming from.

One warning though: if you ask personal questions in an interview, you need to restrict yourself to those that are directly relevant to the needs of the job. Don't get yourself into legal trouble by asking questions contrary to human rights legislation. You must *never* discriminate on the basis of marital status (as well as race, religion, gender, age, etc. Check your local pertinent laws). However, often candidates offer information in an informal way that will give you an indication of the "behind-the-scenes" personality.

b. The Three Dinner Night

I remember trying to make a long-distance decision about hiring a branch sales manager. We had boiled five good candidates down to two. Both came well recommended by the regional sales manager, and both had a good deal of industry experience with a competitor of ours, who had pulled a lot of new business away from our order books. Still, I felt I hadn't gotten to know either of them well enough by mail and by telephone.

I had arranged to meet both candidates and their spouses at different times one evening at my hotel. I thought a quiet drink in the lobby bar or a late evening coffee would be nice. These were intended to be casual encounters that would be followed up by office meetings the next day.

I booked my own flight from our corporate office, scheduling one with a relaxing dinner. In those days, vice presidents flew first class, so the dinner was terrific. When I arrived at the other end, I was comfortably full and just a little mellow from the selection of dinner wines.

As I was checking into guest reception, I heard the familiar voice of the first candidate of the evening. He proudly introduced me to his wife and it soon became apparent that they were expecting to have dinner with me. Not wishing to appear rude or disappoint them, I left my bags at the front desk and off we went to the dining room. My secretary had made the dinner reservations, so I guess I was the one who had screwed up.

While I didn't embark on a full-course meal, I did poke my fork at a lot of delightfully presented items and packed away at least another good helping.

This candidate seemed ideal: well-qualified and with the brightest, most enthusiastic, and supportive spouse you could imagine. It looked like a great marriage providing a solid base for a happy work situation.

I walked them to the lobby, waved goodbye, and started for the bags. Another voice. The second candidate and more introductions. A unique couple to be sure: all ready to have dinner with the vice president from out of town. It was late and they were hungry. They competed for my attention in the elevator and at the hotel dining room table I knew so well. As it happened, the better half was indeed the better half. Had she been the one applying for the job, she would have had it hands down. She had industry management and sales experience

13

(they had met in sales at a competitor) and during the conversation she even indicated that she might like to take a crack at the position. Their relationship lacked glue. They bickered. They were obviously competitive as all get-out. No dice.

I burped my way into the meeting the next day. Candidate number one was easily the better of the two and to my knowledge still leads the company's success in that remote marketplace as I write this book.

My point here is that whenever possible, get to know a little more about your candidates than what's on the application form. **Where they're coming from has a lot to do with where they're going!**

3

Cranking Out the Dreaded Sales Manual

Highlights from a Monday morning executive management meeting: "O.K. Fuller, I think we need a sales manual."

With those words, the crank 'em up motivational bent I was enjoying with our national sales force ground to a near halt and I started a six-month search for weekly excuses on why the manual "wasn't quite ready yet." If you've ever been asked or "volunteered" to think about developing a sales manual from scratch, you know the task can seem like having an enormous elephant to bite into, chew, and swallow.

I suppose it's comparable to making a cold call: it's the fear of the unknown that keeps the project on the back burner. But you *can* eat that whole elephant if you cut it up into little forkfuls of useful information, organize a bit beforehand, and "chapterize" it into logical, progressive hunks.

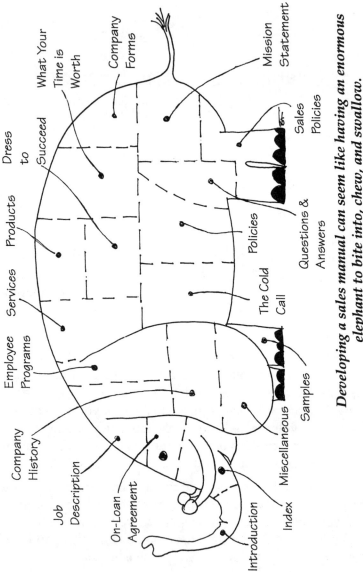

Company History

Job Description

On-Loan Agreement

Introduction

Index

Miscellaneous

Samples

Employee Programs

Services

Products

Dress to Succeed

What Your Time is Worth

Company Forms

The Cold Call

Policies

Questions & Answers

Sales Policies

Mission Statement

Developing a sales manual can seem like having an enormous elephant to bite into, chew, and swallow.

Before you start developing your own how-to manual, you might want to check out what everyone else has filed away. A little background research will make a world of difference. If you belong to a sales management, sales, or marketing organization, you should easily be able to locate colleagues with materials they'll gladly share. If they're generous with their input, you'll quickly get a handle on format, structure, and content, and with amazing speed you'll be able to pull a very usable manual together.

However, before you tackle this task, you need to examine a couple of issues:

(a) Ask yourself why the company needs a sales manual at all. If you have a relatively small sales force of a handful of people, what's the sense? Or what if your sales force is comprised of dealers, distributors, or one person here and one there all over the map? Perhaps instead of developing a sales manual, all you need to structure might be a couple of chapters that can be included in the existing dealer/distributor binder.

(b) Make sure you understand the purpose of developing a sales manual for your organization. Is it —

  (i) a handy job description for salespeople?

  (ii) a textbook for training new recruits?

  (iii) a rule book to keep everyone in line?

  (iv) a substitute for the company's policy manual?

  (v) an image piece for the marketing department?

  (vi) a make-work project?

  (vii) a valuable tool for yourself, a field-sales management team, the next sales manager?

Once you feel confident that a sales manual would be a worthwhile tool in your organization, there are a few organizational steps you can take to help you get started:

(a) Determine the objectives of the manual.

(b) Organize the "chapter titles."

(c) Create a file folder for each chapter.

(d) File any pertinent material in the folders as you come across it.

(e) Organize the materials within each folder.

(f) Work on one chapter at a time.

(g) Introduce each chapter with a couple of descriptive opening paragraphs and keep them brief.

(h) Fill out each chapter after the introduction with point form information. Information prepared and presented in point form, somewhat like this chapter, is easier for the reader to understand — and you can also cover a lot of territory very quickly.

Although I've prepared sales manuals for a number of companies, each quite different for the kinds of business they're in, and although the content of each chapter will obviously take on the unique characteristics of that particular business, the chapter titles can remain pretty much the same.

If your company has already created a corporate policy manual that covers a number of the areas I outline below, you can skip over my suggestions; don't re-invent the wheel. But you can view the following sections as generic sections and chapters that you might wish to customize to help you get started.

a. Introductory Matter

1. On-loan agreement

Include a page that can be signed by the salespeople so they fully understand that the manual is on loan, confidential, and not to be reproduced. You can number each copy of the manual to help protect against copying.

This confidentiality agreement adds importance to the document and communicates the message: "You are a professional salesperson and we are a professional company. We're businesslike and this sales manual is one of our bibles. Please pay attention to the material contained on its pages."

2. Mission statement

I think that right up front your salespeople should understand what their company is all about, its philosophy, and how it has decided to go about doing business. It's a subject that should be addressed early on in the hiring process, but I believe it needs repeating in the sales manual. And I encourage you to have a framed version of it posted in a special place in the reception area of your premises, the staff cafeteria or lounge area, and on an obvious wall in the sales department.

3. Contents page or index

Although a contents or index can go at the front of the manual, don't prepare it until you're done or you'll go nuts trying to work your way through the manual conforming to what you've decided on too early in the creative process.

b. Chapter One: Introduction and Company History

1. Introduction

Here's where you outline the purpose of the sales manual and briefly cover the subject areas you've decided to include. Encourage the reader to be conversant with all parts of the manual and to consider it as a reliable information source of basic company and product facts.

2. Company history

Salespeople should know as much about the company as possible. If your company is an operating subsidiary, or part of a bigger corporation, take time to cover the umbrella organization plus the company the salesperson is representing.

When a salesperson is out in the territory selling to a new customer, a brief outline can serve as a great icebreaker and a warmup to the sales pitch. It's also an ideal place to foster pride and the beginnings of loyalty in the company and it lets the salesperson feel he or she is an important and key part of the bigger picture.

This is the section in which you should include any organizational charts that have been developed, if available.

c. Chapter Two: Products and Services

This is an easy chapter to put together. Outline every product and service you sell and describe each in as much detail as possible.

This is a handy reference area, particularly for new reps. Include descriptive product sheets that might have been produced, photographs, line drawings, sketches — whatever descriptive material you feel best covers the product. You may also wish to include "buzz words" and "industry jargon" that are unique or part of the common language of your business.

The way I have handled this area is to create a "dictionary" based on information (words) collected from all levels of the operation. Don't forget to include in your listing all those "special materials" that are used in the manufacturing process. (Details of the manufacturing process might be worth including as well.)

d. Chapter Three: Company Policies

This section can be divided into two parts: general company policies and sales department policies.

1. General company policies

This section should cover everything from hiring practices, rights, company regulations, hours of operation, and chain-of-command. In short, it outlines what the corporation expects of all its people, not just the sales reps.

2. Sales department policies

Include in this section everything to do with remuneration policies and contractual policies.

(a) Remuneration

(a) The *general policy* the company has set up (straight commission, split commission, salary plus commission, straight salary, etc., or whatever versions you might have in place).

(b) *Commission rates*: Spell them out so there is never a misunderstanding. If various rates are structured for different products, services, or special deals, this is the place for the details.

(c) *Payment of commissions*: When and how reps get paid (i.e., do they get paid following installation? after the company has collected from the customer? on receipt of the order, and then the balance later?)

(d) *Method of payment*: By special check? Along with paycheck? Deposited directly to salesperson's bank account?

(e) *Advances*: What is the company's policy on advancing funds to a salesperson prior to a sale being completed? Is there an emergency situation that the company looks at if the salesperson is in a personal financial jam? When do advances have to be paid back?

(f) *Commissions/special circumstances*: What if a deal gets canceled after a commission is paid? What if an account is reassigned to another rep and deals have been presold? Spell out all the details.

(b) Contractual policies

Under this section, you should outline what the company expects to happen contractually between the company and the customer. Sales reps must understand the legal ramifications of a contractual arrangement so that all details can be clearly spelled out for the customer. Be sure to include samples of all agreements with a simple outline of how they work.

An ideal way to describe each area of a contract might be to illustrate your comments by circling the key parts, numbering that part, and then outlining in detail your concerns. Areas you might consider (depending on the business you're in) include:

- General sale contracts
- Leases
- Lease-purchase agreements
- Maintenance agreements
- Renewal agreements
- Deposits
- Pre-authorized payment plans
- Advanced payment plans

e. Chapter Four: The Professional Sales Executive

Although this is an area that might only be read a couple of times during a rep's career with the company, it serves as an excellent "reminder" section when you want to counsel newer reps or move some of the more individualistic members of the sales force toward bettering their image (and the company's).

This section should include the salesperson's job description in which, of course, you can spell out exactly what is expected of each rep in the context of how your company wants to do business. Think this one through because it can be the basis for solving a number of behavioral problems. I've known sales management teams that have used this area to fire reps. I suppose if you've been brutally honest about the company's level of expectation for its reps and you've regularly communicated these expectations, a deviation from the job description might help you with justifiable grounds for dismissal, should you need them.

You might also check with your company's legal department on this chapter since your expectations must work for the employee as well.

Any job description should include the organizational relationship, primary responsibilities, and expected duties.

Besides using this chapter as a means of providing job descriptions, the following topics are helpful:

(a) Why customers should deal with the company

(b) Checklist of items the rep needs when making a sales call

(c) Planning checklist

(d) What the rep's time is worth

(e) Sales tips (unique to selling your products/services)

(f) Dressing for success

(g) List of logical replies to turn around negative responses to presentations

(h) Sample mockup letters (e.g., followup to sales calls, letters of quotation)

(i) Prospecting tips

(j) Performance evaluation materials

f. Chapter Five: Questions and Answers

When gathering together the information for this area, you should poll everyone within meeting distance in your company. This is a great way to create a company- or sales department-wide brainstorming exercise.

When gathering information, you should make a good attempt to poll most of the departmental management in your company. With each department head, discuss the relevant questions most commonly asked by salespeople and the appropriate responses to those questions. You may also wish to create questions or answers that will help new salespeople understand the particular department in question.

Combine all questions and answers by department. Once you feel comfortable with the collection you've put together, put this chapter aside and revisit it once the whole manual is pretty much set in draft form. Then go through each chapter and make up additional questions, and with your answers, combine them with your first draft of the questions and answers chapter. This chapter then becomes a truly representative compilation of all the facts you would like to get across to your sales reps. It makes a terrific base for later sales training sessions, or works well as an agenda item to pick up a sales meeting. (It's amazing how the seasoned sales pros forget the basics; questions and answers can lead to plenty of interactive discussion.)

Remember to include a good sampling of questions commonly asked by customers with ideal, "company-approved" answers. Keep your questions short and all answers straight and to the point.

You can pull this chapter together just before you finalize your index section. A quick way to put it in order is to go through your draft of the whole sales manual and create brief questions with tight answers. This chapter should be a collection of nearly all the information you present in the manual.

When it comes to sales training exercises or subjects for sales meetings, this can be a great place to pull information for second-time-around reminder sessions.

g. Chapter Six: Cold Call Techniques

Every sales manager I have spoken to on this subject seems to handle it differently, but I strongly recommend that you develop a unique-to-your-company approach and outline it on a step-by-step basis. You might wish to take the reps through a series of scenarios from prospecting, to the first telephone inquiry, and to the physical drop-in cold call.

Your goal in this chapter is to refocus the rep's opinion of cold calling from a fearful one to a satisfactory exercise using formulas already considered successful in your organization.

h. Chapter Seven: Miscellaneous

This chapter, a collect-all for forms, miscellaneous information, etc. is an important and logical concluding section to your sales manual. Be sure to include a covering, descriptive piece so the reader is completely comfortable with the materials you've bound in.

4

Quick and Dirty
Sales Training

In his book, *The First-Time Sales Manager* (Self-Counsel Press), Theodore Tyssen tells us that training salespeople means helping them acquire job-related skills, with the emphasis on the skills that make people more productive in selling. He says that learning a skill without putting it to work on the job is just knowledge acquisition, and that a skill isn't really a skill unless it is *actively practiced in real job situations.*

I agree. And who is better suited as a trainer than an in-house pro who has developed all the skills right on the firing line and who also has a developed knack for passing on the skills?

You'll find that in most instances, some of the best trainers are hidden away in your own sales department. My style of sales management is to delegate some of the training to the old hands. Not the old hands with the old war stories and the so-so sales, but the old hands who are star performers. Out of the top 20% who produce 80% of your business, you'll find some unique personalities who are not teachers, and you'll probably spot a couple of steady producers who "always have the time" to help their peers grow.

Let's assume your new sales reps know all they need to know about the products or services the company has to offer. Let's assume you've selected the reps for all the right reasons and you're comfortable with your decision to bring them on-board. Then it's time to see them move into the action. So now what do you do?

a. Pro-Partnering

Pro-partnering is a system of partnering a new rep with a seasoned pro. Without interrupting the schedules of your superstars (and with their full cooperation), make sure the new reps spend as much time as possible on the firing line with the best shooters in your sales department. A week in a pro-partnering exercise will give trainees ample time to experience a variety of situations, client types, problem-solving challenges, and perhaps even observe a couple of cold calls. It's not necessary for trainees to spend the whole week with the same rep; move them around if possible to provide a variety of real situations handled in different ways.

All the time the trainees are partnered, they will see how a pro organizes time, opens and closes deals, and communicates with the sales department, the plant, or other behind-the-scenes support teams. If you have made good partnering choices, you will probably see an additional benefit of the trainee developing a couple of mentors within the ranks. Your trainees now have people to bounce ideas and problems off; trusted colleagues that they can count on.

At the end of each pro-partnering day, ask your trainees to write an observation report describing what worked, what didn't, and why. If you've have only one trainee to be concerned with, you can review these reports one-on-one, but if more than one rep is being trained, it is preferable to hold a review in a group session.

b. Observation and Role-play

Another very effective training exercise, especially when used close on the heels of the pro-partnering observation phase, is the use of role-play scenarios. These serve as ideal rehearsals for those important first days out.

One way to create these scenarios is to make scriptwriting and role-playing the themes of a sales meeting. Depending on the size of your group, break the sales force into groups of two, three, or four and have each group create a skit depicting a particular situation that one of them has run into and that everyone can relate to.

Once all of the teams have created a situation, have them pass their notes on to another team for role-playing. If you can, videotape these role-plays and have the whole department critique the exercise before moving along to the next group.

Following the sales meeting, work a number of these scenarios into a training session and repeat the exercises with your trainees using a combination of the notes you kept and the videotape.

28

5

Cranking Up
Your Presentations

As a sales management executive, you'll be called upon time and time again to make presentations to a broad range of audience types. These might include both management above and below your level, to peer groups, to your company's corporate head office personnel, to your sales team at perhaps local, regional, and national events, and possibly to colleagues in sales and marketing organizations you might be part of.

And there will be plenty of opportunities to present, usually in concert with one of your representatives, to key clients, established and new.

Although the best presentations are usually those planned well in advance, often you'll be in a position where "you're on deck" within a couple of short hours. If you understand and practice the basics of good presentation skills, you'll be better equipped to successfully sell your position, your ideas, or your goods to your audience.

And once you feel comfortable with pulling the presentation rabbit out of the briefcase hat on shorter than average notice, you should plan a sales meeting around the subject to pass on your skills to the team.

The fact is, it seems like there's always a presentation to be made. A couple of years ago I was asked by the government to create and customize a special program for a unique audience comprised of senior bureaucrats holding the responsibilities for running the day-to-day operations of the departments of corrections, emergency preparedness, police services, motor vehicles, and the chief coroner's office. Because of the nature of their business, they were logical media targets when anything dramatic and new happened in their various areas of responsibility.

Things like jail breaks, floods, earthquakes, law enforcement issues, licensing changes, and unexplained tragedies tend to get a lot of attention from reporters and a concerned public. To respond to any issues at hand, presentations had to be made and public sector management had to fully appreciate the skills involved to effectively sell their positions.

My communications company was contracted to develop media and presentation skills training programs. Suzanne Sherkin and I wrote two reference publications to accompany the classroom session.

So here in a nutshell are some ideas for making great presentations. The following material is adapted from the two publications I wrote for government spokepeople: *Media Skills Notebook* and *Presentation Skills Notebook*.

a. Be A Performer and A Facilitator

Think of your presentation as a performance on a stage. You are the lead actor. Everything you say is crucial and your appearance and gestures are important.

When you make a presentation, you are selling. You're selling your concepts, your opinions, your credibility, and your organization. You want the audience to believe in you and to pay attention. You may have captive bodies, but not necessarily captive minds.

The first thing you as a presenter must do is get attention and arouse interest, then you must maintain that attention and interest throughout the session. *You want an alert and receptive audience.* After all, your goal is to crank 'em up!!!

It's much easier to conduct a lively meeting than a dull one. The lively meeting moves and picks up momentum as it goes. It generates enthusiasm that wins spontaneous applause for you. This is one of the most generous rewards an audience can pay. With an interested audience, you don't have to fight so hard to win acceptance for the ideas you're trying to convey.

As presenter, you are the entertainment for the duration of the program. Get into the role: believe in what you're saying, care about it, and convince everyone else of the importance and credibility of it. You have a responsibility to your audience to do a great job. Their time is as valuable as yours.

b. Know Your Audience

Confidence is knowledge. The more you know about the people you're dealing with and what their needs and expectations are, the better off you'll be. Each audience will have a slightly different agenda to be met. Know their concerns, problems, interests, and expectations. If you know them, you'll know how to get the maximum attention and interest.

During your presentation, use the new information you learned about individual members. Flavor your presentation with personal references to audience members; make your points of information directly relevant to them. This will keep your presentation from looking "canned" — a syndrome of oft-presented shows. People can tell when a speaker is just going through the motions and repeating tired, old information.

31

Be aware of your audience's nonverbal communication, especially body language. Are people looking at their watches? Is anybody fidgeting, doodling, yawning, sitting with crossed arms and legs, talking, glancing at the window or door, or looking bored and distracted? Address your presentation to those members who are not being fully attentive. Try to make eye contact with them. Move so you can face them if you are on a stage or podium. Walk closer to them if you can mill around the audience. Say something creative or fresh that you know (because of your preparation work beforehand) will grab their attention. If you've been droning on in a monotonous tone of voice, snap out of it and vary your pitch effectively. Your goal is to have everyone's full interest and respect.

c. Be Prepared

Be organized and well prepared. Have all of your visual material clearly labelled so you don't have to fumble around for it. The audience is likely to remember the distractions more than the subject content. REHEARSE! REHEARSE! Prepare well in advance whenever possible. Don't wing it!

1. Scout out the location

Being prepared means being aware of the entire situation and feeling comfortable in the role of technician.

Before you're due to make your presentation, scout out the room. Get a feel for it. Consider its shape and size and where you will be in relation to the audience. Is there a podium at the front? Will you be able to comfortably circulate throughout the room?

You'll probably want to use visual images, so determine where they will be shown. If there is already a screen, pull it down and make sure it's in good shape. If there is no screen, make sure there is a large, white wall that will provide an unobscured background for the visuals. Arrange the seating in such a way that once people are seated, no one's head will interfere with a view of you or the projected image.

2. Use visual images

Every presentation is enhanced by the use of visual images. Visuals give the audience a break from having to concentrate solely on you and your voice, while giving you a break from having to be the only form of entertainment.

You have a variety of choices when considering how to present your visuals: 35 mm slides, overhead acetates, flip charts, and white or black boards. Each choice requires a slightly different approach to your presentation and creates a different atmosphere. For instance, flip charts and overhead projectors work well with small groups, while 35 mm slides on a large screen can create a colorful presentation for large audiences. If you have time, try out different equipment choices to see which ones fit your own personal style and presentation content.

3. Keep your graphics simple and clear

Whatever presentation method you choose for your graphics, keep all visuals simple, clear, and informative. Don't clutter them up with too much color or written information. Avoid excessive detail. An audience can't absorb it in the short time a visual is on the screen. Whether you're using 35 mm slides or overhead transparencies, the same principles of good design apply. Ask a designer for advice or get a book on basic design principles. Each visual should include information about one idea at a time and contain the essence of that idea.

There are a myriad of design rules for the use of color and type. Your job is to present the information well; leave the graphics job to graphics professionals.

If you have an art department or special staff resource people who can make full creative use of a variety of designer/artist software packages on the market, then you have those "graphics professionals" in-house.

I've found that slides are really ticklers or prompters for the presenter and do not work well if they are covered with the text from a full speech. My presentations have worked particularly well when I combined simple artwork, graphs, and cartoon illustrations with just a handful of words. I like to keep the backgrounds in darker tones and the graphics in bright, colorful, powerfully strong hues. Copy seems to work better if you use reverse type (white letters on a black background) and a serif typeface (when the letters have little hooks at the ends, like Courier or Times — see below for specific examples).

This is a serif typeface — Times

This is a sans serif typeface — Avant Garde

4. Know about technical requirements

Know how to use all of the equipment needed for your presentation and be prepared to handle on-the-spot breakdowns. Things always seem to happen when you're the least prepared, so be sure to ask technicians to show you how to use all the equipment. Make sure all the needed supplies, such as extension cords, extra bulbs, or chalk, are handy.

If your equipment does break down, be prepared to carry on using only your notes. You may want to have handouts ready for such an occasion. When a technical breakdown occurs, deal with it openly. Let your audience know what's happening and try to handle it with as much grace as possible. Undoubtedly, many people in the audience will have experienced similar situations. After you've acknowledged what's happening, get on with your presentation.

See Checklist #1 at the end of this chapter and use it to make sure all of the above is taken care of.

d. Prepare Your Script

When organizing your presentation, make an outline of your subject rather than writing a script word for word. Think about the visual possibilities while you're writing your script. The whole presentation should flow and integrate the key points.

By the time you have expanded an outline, designed your visuals, and rehearsed the main points, you should be familiar enough with the topic to be able to speak easily and eloquently using your slides as backup support only.

e. Speak Your Script, Don't Read It

How you speak is key to getting your message across. Rehearse your comments to be sure you know the material and to practice intonation. Voice inflections and intonation make all the difference to how well the meaning is conveyed. Enthusiastic, animated speech is far more effective than monotone speech.

Speak at a moderate, lively pace. The audience will lose interest if you speak too quickly or too slowly. Nervous presenters are often guilty of quick-talk. If you're nervous, concentrate on articulating each word to slow you down.

Don't read your script. Speak it. Be as casual and personable as possible, making direct eye contact with members of the audience. There's nothing more ineffective than someone *reading* a presentation.

f. Be On Time

Of course, no one would ever plan on being late for a presentation, but arriving just on time for the beginning isn't much better. Plan on being early, which means giving yourself enough time to comfortably set up, without rushing, and be done with all the organizing *before* the audience members begin arriving.

Being on time also means beginning *and* ending on schedule. Don't ruin a successful presentation by ending late.

g. Be Confident

Confidence is the key to your success. If you've done your homework, you won't feel intimidated or unsure about anything because you will have covered everything. That includes researching your subject thoroughly, being informed about your audience, and feeling confident about the technicalities of the presentation itself. The more secure you feel, the more confident you'll be. And the more confident you are, the better, more creative your presentation.

> IF YOU KNOW YOURSELF, YOUR SUBJECT,
> YOUR AUDIENCE, AND YOUR VENUE,
> YOUR PRESENTATION WILL CRANK 'EM UP!!!

Checklist #1
Presentation Checklist

☑ Check the location thoroughly.

☑ Locate all electrical outlets.

☑ Confirm that lights and/or blinds can be manipulated for the proper light levels.

☑ Bring a spare extension cord.

☑ Confirm that all necessary furniture will be available to you (e.g., table for projector, enough chairs for audience).

☑ Make certain you have the right equipment and confirm that it's in good working order.

☑ Make certain you know how to attend to minor breakdowns.

☑ In case all your equipment fails, have plans so you can easily carry on.

☑ Make sure all of your visual and speaking materials are carefully organized.

☑ Carry a watch so you can ensure your presentation begins and ends on time.

☑ Make sure that you are dressed comfortably and appropriately for the presentation.

☑ If you're nervous, do some breathing and stretching exercises.

6

Winging It When You Have To: Meetings In Minutes

It happens. It could be a screw up in scheduling or your well-planned meeting might have been structured around one important speaker, topic, or movie and something terrible happens (or maybe you were on the road solving a crisis, taking your mind away from that Monday sales meeting to prepare for).

Sales meetings, or any meetings for that matter, should be planned well ahead of time whenever possible, but there might be many times in your management career when you just don't have the luxury of preplanning time.

In other parts of this book I mention that my management style has always been participatory. This means getting my audience on side to the extent that they get to sing and dance along with me.

What better action could you plan for than to have your sales team take over your sales meeting while you just sit back and play the role of master facilitator of ceremonies. When it comes to winging it, a participatory leadership style means that you really do little more than encourage guidelines, set the tone, and allow your audience to present to themselves.

The purpose of this chapter isn't to point you down the road of last minute planning, but instead to pass along a quick meeting agenda template that you can customize to fit your requirements.

This style has evolved over many years of observing fidgeting audiences tired of listening to a boss drone on. So what better action could you plan for than to have the audience take over your meeting while you just sit back and play emcee?

If you're really stuck in a last minute crisis, you can always delegate the running of the meeting to your most senior salesperson, or rotate from one rep to another (yet another way to develop inside talent).

And now for some thoughts on sales meetings.

a. Sales Meetings

1. When?

When should you hold sales meetings? I don't believe you should have sales meetings if you have nothing to communicate. I do believe that as a sales manager you'll have plenty to say; therefore you should plan to have meetings on a regular basis.

Generally, Monday mornings are the best time of the week to have your sales meeting. An early get-together tends to kick start the business week into higher gear and move aside the weekend yawns. If you hold the meeting later in the week, it can get buried in other things. Monday morning is the ideal time to remind everyone of what to expect during the five work days ahead, such as any changes in the organization, or any big deals that are closing, and so on.

If everyone knows ahead of time that a regular meeting takes place on Monday morning, they can plan their calls accordingly. They can set aside the whole morning for office work like checking up on orders placed, troubleshooting with the factory, discussing a dental plan problem with administration, getting the call reports from last week in and, of course, structuring appointments over the next few days. Basically, they can clear their plates for the week of selling ahead.

2. How long?

From my experience, your meetings should be no longer than an hour. The one exception is if you are attaching a sales training session to it, introducing a special guest speaker who requires more time, or kicking off a detailed contest. But even in these situations you should make an honest attempt to keep your meeting to that magic 60 minutes so audience attention doesn't lag.

3. At what time?

The earlier the better. Although I'm not an early bird myself, I've always pushed for an 8:00 a.m. or 8:30 a.m. start time. Later in the morning means you have to pull people off the telephones or away from other tasks they've created for themselves.

End of day meeting times are difficult because you'll get people hanging around after lunch "between things," and then half of what you've told them at the meeting will be forgotten by the next morning. The exception to this is the timing for a contest kickoff. The best times I've ever experienced were held at midpoints in the afternoon (3:00 p.m. to 4:00 p.m.) and they carried through to the early evening and usually included a theme dinner.

4. Dealing with latecomers

Usually, it is the same few people who arrive in the nick-of-time or late. One of my bosses, the company owner, was reputed to have locked the meeting room doors the minute the meeting was to begin. His reputation preceded him to most meetings he called and rarely was there a late entrant. Discretion and fairness must guide you in how you handle this one.

I do ask for the door to be closed on the minute so that the latecomer will get the message as will the gathered group. A subtle way of handling tardiness is to put a handmade note on the meeting room door saying: "If you are arriving late for this meeting, please enter as quietly as possible with the least amount of interruption to everyone else who cared enough to arrive on time!"

b. Winging It

There may be times when you have no choice but to wing it through a meeting. But remember, the secret to winging a sales meeting is — *you don't really wing it.* In your sales meeting files, always keep a couple of "preplanned meetings" ready to go. These don't have to be full-blown, detailed agendas, but reasonably structured plans with a couple of general areas that can be filled in by your audience (this is where delegation and participatory management of the meetings come into play).

Sample #1 shows an example of an agenda with breakdown of each area to be covered that can be used time and time again. Sample #2 shows a simplified version you can use on an overhead acetate, complete with the company's logo. If you use the overhead version, you'll come across as being particularly well organized. At the same time, you're winging it!

c. Agenda Fillers

Using the basic agenda format shown in Samples #1 and #2, you should be able to run any sales meeting and make it effective. Here are a few "thought starters" for subjects you might wish to slot into the fourth agenda item called Special. Remember to keep the total meeting time to one hour, so make adjustments to other agenda items when necessary.

1. Videos, films, slides, and overheads

Any visual aid can improve a presentation or meeting. Think of including materials created within your own organization.

Since virtually everyone today has access to, and can easily use camcorders, you could arrange to show some videotaped pieces. These could include subject matter such as customer service, production, new products, and competitive or market-place-oriented information. If you've saved any videos from your role-playing session (the older ones could be quite comical and meaningful), these could give a terrific lift to a meeting.

You can also rent good visual materials through training organizations, publishing houses, and video rental stores. Many have well-stocked business libraries with strong sales and motivational materials on hand. Libraries are another good source. Your local public library may have material appropriate for your use, and colleges and universities often maintain excellent business libraries. If you have a connection through a professor or lecturer, or if one of your people is taking an extension program, you should be able to access videos and films.

Agenda

1. **Welcome**
   - new faces, old faces returning
   - out-of-town reps if in
   - visitors to meeting
   - housekeeping thoughts
   - agenda overview

2. **Last week in review**
   - have each person write down the three most important sales activities that happened over the last week (e.g., key sales, cold calls, situation developing a client, etc.)
   - each person outlines a point followed by group discussion

3. **Headaches and hangups**
   - solving problems and turning them into opportunities
   - group discussion

4. **Special**
   - present guest (if applicable)
   - introduction and background
   - guest comments
   - video/film/other stuff

5. **Announcements**
   - product information
   - deliveries
   - notice board type of information (social)
   - other departments' announcements

6. **Close**
   - thanks for participation today
   - reminders
   - next week's meeting time

Agenda

1. Welcome

2. Last week in review

3. Headaches and hangups

4. Special

5. Announcements

6. Close

2. Guests

Bringing in a guest to the sales department meeting can benefit your group in different ways. You can invite customers who like the company and have the right chemistry (and time) to brainstorm on ideas to improve service.

A "meet the manager" session can be organized by bringing in people from other departments within your organization. Department heads, supervisory staff, or key staff can be brought in to explain their end of the business. This creates a win-win situation for all parties concerned. Often, other parts of your company are not aware of the personalities, problems, situations, and client issues that percolate in the sales department. As well, your guest's presentation will generally shed a great deal of light on other corners of the firm, so this time can be illuminating for everyone.

Suppliers to your industry can also bring a strong background of product knowledge in their specific area. If your reps are now selling products that are proprietary in nature, it makes good sense for everyone to understand where the supplier is coming from.

3. Role-play and skits

Role-playing sessions, when done well, almost always work. If possible, prepare realistic sales scenarios prior to your meeting, have the criteria for the role-play outlined in brief point form, then randomly select a few "volunteers." Ask them to leave the room for five minutes to get their act together. While they're away, discuss the criteria briefing notes you gave them with the group still in the room.

Although role-plays can be quite humorous at times, you must keep the participants focused and on track to reap the greatest benefits. If you can, videotape the sessions for replay and critiquing purposes just following the live action.

Ask everyone to take notes: this will help them to focus and give you plenty of areas in which to lead discussion.

4. The competition

Create a panel from a randomly selected group of the sales force and have them move to the front of the room. Let them become the "experts" on the competition, fielding questions from the rest of your team and reporting on what's going on with the competitive forces in the field.

5. Brainstorming sessions

Brainstorming is always an effective means of generating new ideas and solving problems. Use Worksheet #3, the Brainstorming Matrix, to facilitate discussion on a variety of topics.

Sales meetings are excellent forums in which to explore and brainstorm various subjects with your whole sales team. Remember, many heads are better than one. With your photocopier, enlarge the Brainstorming Matrix and produce it on an acetate sheet for use on an overhead projector.

As sales manager, facilitate the discussion of an important issue or problem and encourage your team's involvement in helping uncover details, your objective being to fully explore the subject. For instance, let's say you were discussing cold calling (a subject most sales managers like to bring to their sales meeting agendas every now and then).

Using the matrix to examine this subject, insert cold calling into the middle box (main idea). Then extend your thinking along into secondary categories and then to as many sub-categories as you need to create.

A secondary category might be "New Accounts" or "Preparing for the cold call" or "What to say" or "Getting past the secretary."

As a working example let's extend, from the secondary category, "Preparing for the cold call" to a sub-category called "The Sales Kit." For all the categories, develop a great deal of interactive discussion and fill in additional highlights on the matrix.

From this brief mind mapping example you can see how a subject can be explored fully and quickly, right in front of your sales force.

Later on in this book you will see a number of examples of how mind map matrixes effectively spell out the whole planning sequence of contest ideas.

Worksheet #3
Brainstorming Matrix

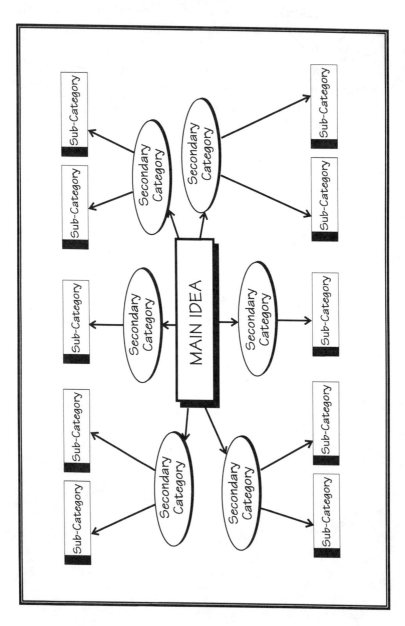

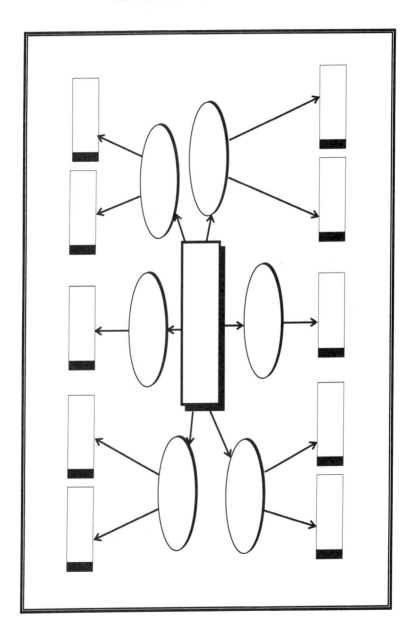

7

The Professor of Antonology's Team-Building Exercise

You may be asking yourself why you need to read a chapter on team building; after all, isn't that what you've already done — built a team of sales reps to sell a product or service? Unless you're directing a national sales force with reps far afield, you probably know virtually everyone on your sales team and have their resumes, profiles, and personal files up-to-date and close at hand. And you've probably already run some sales promotional programs within the sales team and feel you've got a handle on the group as a whole and the dynamics of what makes them move together.

So why team building? Why now?

The meaning of the term team building can take a number of twists if you think about it. For instance, it can mean any or all of the following:

- Building a better team

- Bringing the team together so everyone can work with each other as they head for one common goal

- Developing a group team spirit

- Getting team members on-side so they know the strengths of their peers and who they can count on

So team building is another way that you, as sales manager, can crank up your sales force. You can build a better team, you can help them work together more effectively, you can promote a healthy spirit among them, and you can see the positive results of a group of reps working cooperatively and collectively.

The following exercise that I once used can be used by you to creatively crank up your team.

a. The Professor of Antonology

I was poking around a toy store a couple of years ago (a favorite place of mine for getting ideas) and I spotted a box of little black plastic ants near the cash register. I had been looking for something totally different to introduce a team-building exercise to a government client and recalled some private sector friends commenting that working with the government must be like working with ants.

The store only had a dozen or so ants in stock so I tracked down the ant supplier, an importer with thousands of the little guys. Apparently the ants were popular items among nasty kids who planned practical jokes on their parents and teachers. The plastic toys appeared perfectly ant-sized, and from a quick glance, identical to the real picnic biters.

I bought a couple of thousand ants (since this is the only way to get them at the wholesale price) and packed up a few hundred for my client visit. I should tell you that my client was the Attorney General and the team-building exercise was scheduled for senior level prosecutors — a serious bunch.

I thought I'd do a little research on the humble ant and found out some amazing things to use in meetings. First, as everyone probably knows, ants have tremendous strength for their size, and together, they can accomplish amazing feats. (Like a good team perhaps?) They are also tenacious; they just don't give up. (Does this mean that a sales ant always gets the order?)

Ants can venture far, far from the anthill, go about their serious business of collecting food (or making sales without supervision), and make it back with the goods no matter what the odds. And they are fearsome critters. Some are aggressive, while others are relatively passive — until they're riled. Then watch out.

Ants are incredibly honest. You can see what they are doing; take them at ant-face value and act accordingly. They are immensely loyal to their sales manager — the queen — and will give their lives for both her and their ant sales department back at the colony. They're hard to squash, and although mortally wounded, will drag a scrap of bread or their sample case back to the nest for everyone else.

So with this information in hand, I took my ants to the team-building meeting. My client agreed to give me some free rein in order to pull his group together, get them liking each other a little more, and motivate them to head in the same direction.

I believe that one of the first things you must do when you conduct the first team-building exercise is get to know where the members of your audience are coming from. The best way to do this is to ask each person to tell the group about himself or herself.

b.   The Professor's Interview Technique...with Ants

When I arrived at the early morning meeting, I noticed that coffee, juice, and iced water were available and fancy little plates heaped with fresh muffins covered the side table. I strategically placed a few of the ants around the food before the participants arrived. And on the conference table, one per person, were note pads and pencils. I placed one ant on each note pad.

When the participants filed in, there were a few snickers heard and the odd reference to the ants. I thought to myself what a wonderful time I was in for.

I closed the conference room door and my client hit the light switch. The room went black. In the dark I had heaped a couple of hundred ants on the overhead projector glass, then switched on the projector. The ants on the screen had grown a few inches...but they were really realistic.

I started to talk about the ants, and as I covered some of the basic facts learned about them, with a sharpened pencil, I moved them from a large, disorganized mass to highly regimented and regulated team structures. I touched on the obvious comparisons between ants as individuals with all their strengths and weaknesses, and ants as team players with all their additional strengths. I explained how what was happening on the overhead projector glass could be applied to the participants' situation in the workplace.

I lay the pencil down on the glass for a moment and said, "You know, if this pencil were made of chocolate, it would be an attractive find for an ant out on food-search patrol, but there's no way that ant could get it back to the anthill. But with a little communication with the other ants, they could all form an army to work together to get that chocolate pencil to the nest. And they'd all eat.

Now the ant has to know who to communicate with, the needs of the rest of the ant colony, and where others are coming from. They are a true team. *Like every one of you in this room!*

Let's find out who our ants are and where they're coming from so we can work closer together as a team."

With that, on came the lights. Virtually everyone in the room was playing with a little black plastic ant. The ice was broken. There was already a feeling of team.

c. The Professor of Antonology's Interview Process

If you use the ant exercise, you need to keep the rhythm going after your introduction. When the lights go on, divide the group up into twos. Ask each person to conduct a three-minute interview with his or her neighbor to the left, and then reverse the roles for another three to four minutes. All interviews take place at the same time, so the room is filled with ice-breaking chatter.

You can put questions on the overhead to help direct the interviews if you wish. Sample #3 shows a few examples; of course, feel free to customize them as you see fit. After about ten minutes, wind the interviews down and then go around the room asking each person to tell the others about his or her neighbor.

As a team-building exercise, the combination "ant-and-interview" session works very well with any group. It is a terrific ice-breaker and meeting starter, and if you remember not to rush the process, you'll get a lot more out of it.

Task: a quick interview of your neighbor, then switch roles.

Time limit: approximately 3 minutes each.

Please find out:

1. The person's name
(real one)

2. Job and responsibility
(what he or she thinks it is)

3. Background
(the neat stuff)

4. Key personal achievement
(business or pleasure)

5. Hobby/favorite sporting activity
(you don't have to tell everything!)

6. Why your neighbor is here and what
personal objective he or she has set
for the day.

d. And One Last Use for Those Ants...

I always carry a few of my ants in an envelope in my briefcase. I find them an excellent way to start or finish a new-client presentation. As a consultant I'm constantly on the look-out for new business, which boils down to "helping clients build better anthills!" I usually work this into the pitch for business and leave an ant behind.

I continue the theme by gluing an ant beside my signature on the "thanks-for-meeting-with-me-to-talk" letter I send out as a follow up.

And just one other thing. The ants cause a riot if strategically placed on a salmon roll at a sushi bar.

8

The Attitude Sales Meeting

a. Attitude

You've seen it on bumper stickers and read about the success major organizations have had with it. You've heard about winning athletes who have got winning ones, and of course as customers, we've all run into businesses with really bad ones.

I'm sure many a time you've closed your office door behind someone and walked back to your desk muttering, "I've got to do something about that attitude!"

Attitude. As the bumper sticker says, "Attitude is everything!" It's so true.

As a sales management professional, a key ingredient in how you crank 'em up might first be to have a good look at where your salespeople are coming from, where they are today, and where they're headed. In the last chapter, I addressed a couple of good ways of getting a handle on this area by playing the role of the Professor of Antonology. If you use those techniques, you need to understand your team members' backgrounds, their needs, and their objectives as individuals and as a group. Once you understand all that, you'll be much better-equipped to motivate them to sales successes without budgetary boundaries.

In 1986 something happened to me that changed my attitude about a lot of things. I met Laurie Skreslet, internationally noted for his "special attitude." The first Canadian in history to summit the world's highest mountain, he asked me if I'd help him with a new group that had formed to try Everest from the Chinese side, via the Tibetan access and the North Col route over the Rongbuk Glacier. The experiences I shared on this wonderfully adventurous expedition have long remained with me, and they can easily be assimilated into an approach for digging up more business.

Becoming a support team member of the highly successful Everest Light Expedition, I joined a group of motivated people attempting yet another human assault on Mount Everest. I had previously done a little social climbing, but travelling up a mountain in anything less luxurious than a chair lift or heated gondola, let alone grunting up the mother mountain of them all, was something I wouldn't have considered seriously.

But the team was going to do it. They were determined to prepare themselves for Everest, get through a politically nervous China, then through Tibet (which was hostile to China), and then to Everest.

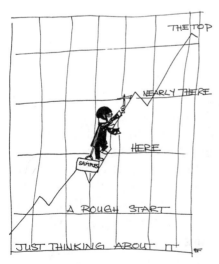

Climbing to the top of Everest — simple. Ha! But they were cranked up, fortified with ample helpings of *attitude*.

It's probably not such a new idea to adopt the analogy of a mountain climbing expedition to a sales task, a perfect theme on which to structure the creative platform for a sales contest. Normally for me, after meeting someone like Laurie Skreslet, I would have huddled away with a group of sales managers and developed a "Climb Your Mountain" or "Peak Your Quota" sales contest.

In this case, the fundraising part of the climb was the priority. No money meant no costly permits from the Chinese Mountaineering Society, no travel, no food, no equipment, and no Yak drivers to tote the loads to Camp One. Jim Elzinga, the Everest Light Expedition team leader, along with many of the team members, had approached a great number of logical corporate sponsor prospects.

Seeing the ideal marketing and promotional opportunities, and knowing the team had a good shot at accomplishing their objectives, many suppliers committed to sponsorship with goods or services. Obtaining all of the needed items was great, but we needed cash.

I encouraged Jim to apply a theme to his corporate presentation in order to attract sponsors. I suggested that he offer the sponsors the concept of a climbing theme where they could buy into the expedition with cash, and their people could buy into increasing their business.

In Jim's studio, I fixed a ten-foot piece of "no-seam" background paper to his wall and on it I sketched in a huge mountain topped with the prospect's corporate flag. At the far left lower extremity of the paper, I wrote the name of the prospect he was meeting with the next day, Continental Bank. I drew a line along the bottom of the paper to the mountain, divided the line into various points of reference, then created a number of camps up the north side approach Jim had planned for the assault on Everest.

The marks indicated sales target levels. I knew that Continental Bank was no different from any other kind of business. They wanted new business. They wanted to do more business with their existing customers, and they wanted to introduce new services and expand on ones they already had. Each of the points on the mountain represented a target for them — just like the objectives for the climbers.

So Jim went into his meeting with Continental Bank to sell them on the attitude of winning, of summitting their sales mountains, on the attitude the climbers have, and of summitting Everest. He took his climbing gear and his attitude and he sold the deal. Continental Bank became the key financial organization supporting the Everest Light Expedition. And their corporate logo really did make it to the top of Everest.

Climbers have great attitude and Laurie Skreslet and Jim Elzinga seemed totally focused on how we all moved toward the summit years before fixing the ropes to the advance camps.

b. Putting Attitude Into Your Sales Meeting

When I returned to North America after my adventure with the Everest Light Expedition, I tried to figure out what the word attitude meant to me and how I could apply what I had experienced firsthand to the world of business marketing.

I've found that the attitude theme makes for a most interesting sales meeting core item, either all by itself or as the beginning portion to a longer session.

The way I like to manage sales meetings is to let the sales people take some ownership of the get-together. I work out an agenda, then isolate parts of it to involve them, and really get some interaction going.

In the case of the Attitude Sales Meeting, I bring up a series of overheads onto the screen and then lead a discussion, making sure that each and every person in the room is invited to put his or her two cents in. On each overhead is a key word that provokes dialogue, then together we wing it.

You can do the same. Take the graphics that are reproduced on the next few pages, copy them onto plain white paper, and enlarge them on your copier. With a minimal amount of touching up, (maybe you'd like to add your company logo, your sales team's name, or if you're tying it in with a contest theme, the themed graphics you've developed) you can reproduce them on overhead acetates.

The next step is to script your own version of my comments about each of the letters in the word "attitude," customized of course to your team's specific requirements. Each letter in the word represents one or more key discussion points. These lead to brief comments that are in turn easily applied to almost any unique circumstances.

There may be a lot of ways to break up the individual letters in the word "attitude," and I've put together a version that you can use. *But it only works if you present it with attitude!*

Attitude

Acceptance
Team
Training
Interest
Tenacity
Understanding
Dedication
Excellence

Acceptance

1. A is for Acceptance

Use the following for discussion notes directed to your roomful of sales people.

- Do you think that any of us can be successful if we're not happy with who we are? Who we are right now?

- If you're sitting here at this meeting questioning why you're in sales at all, it'll show on your face. Your body language won't work for you, your poor attitude will come through in your voice, and you'll be cheating yourself out of making half the sale. You must **accept** who you are right now, before you can decide with any honesty which direction you're headed in.

- Before you sell any goods (or services), you must sell yourself. If you can't accept that you're a salesperson, then neither can your customer. So if you know the first "product" — yourself — and you're happy with who you are and accept who you are, then you're probably a long way into making the sale.

- Let's talk about it...(and go around the room, asking individuals what the word acceptance means to them).

- Acceptance also means accepting the company and the company's products you're selling. It means embracing new ideas, concepts, directions, innovations, and products with enthusiasm. It means not just accepting them with a nod, but with a full burst of energy.

Team

2. T is for Team

Unless you're running a one-person show, the sales department is usually, or at least should be, a team. Here's your chance to introduce a team-building component to the meeting. Discuss something simple like, "Why are two heads better than one?" Then pass out blank pieces of paper to everyone and get them to list how many uses they can come up with for a newspaper. A minute or two should be plenty.

Get them to quickly total what they've written. Add up all the numbers and divide by the number of people participating in the exercise. You'll come up with an average per person.

Then get the group to break into twos. Have them do the exercise once again, but this time discussing the subject between the two of them and adding together their numbers. Again get the totals. It will be easily noted that the average will have increased.

Another exercise to exemplify the importance of the team is "the trust fall." It's also a great way to mix up the meeting a bit and get people moving around.

Get everyone to form a circle. Put one person in the middle, hands clasped in front and eyes blindfolded. Now ask that person to fall backwards, letting one or more members of the circle catch him or her.

Trust in the team is evident and you can generate ample discussion on how it relates to selling and working together within the sales department. You might also wish to bring the rest of the company into the picture. Remind the people from other departments that while the sales department is a team unto themselves, they are still part of a bigger team: the rest of the company.

I've found it of terrific benefit to bring people from other parts of the organization into sales meetings as special guests. And the attitude theme is perfect for outsiders as well.

Training

3.   T is for Training

Training never stops. And if it does, your efforts with the sales department will fail. The most experienced of athletes, winners, and doers train, train, and train. And continue to train. To win, they constantly develop new skills and hone them to razor-sharp perfection.

For the climbers in the Everest Light Expedition, the training was always ongoing. Jim Elzinga told me he had struck a deal with the operators of one of the highest free-standing towers in the world, The CN Tower in Toronto, Canada. Almost every day he jogged the hundreds of stairway sections to the top, and then to the bottom, and then to the top again.

Discuss with your sales people how they feel about training, what programs they might know about, and if they are interested in participating. You might also use the opportunity to discuss a new training program, or training materials that have been budgeted into your plan.

Here, too, is a chance to discuss the training that goes on within the company in other areas. It's good for the sales department to understand the ongoing educational programs that are benefitting the rest of the company team.

Interest

4. I is for Interest

- Do your sales people take a sincere interest in themselves? In the company's future?

- Are they interested in their customers as individuals? Their customers' needs?

- Are they interested in knowing about the competition? What do they know now?

- Are they interested in the history of their company? The history of a product?

Ask them about interest. What does the word mean to them as it relates to selling? Do your sales people come in, "punch a time clock," pick up their samples, and hit the streets? Discuss their interest level and how it can affect their success.

Tenacity

5. T is for Tenacity

Ask your sales team: "Do you stick with things?"

The Everest Light Expedition climbers did. It was amazing to see how tenacious each person was. Over the years spent planning the climb, there must have been hundreds and hundreds of little setbacks. Problems that seemed difficult to handle at the time became challenging opportunities. They could have pulled the plug hundreds of times. But they wanted to summit that mountain and they hung on to the dream and wouldn't let go.

Ask your salespeople how tenacious they are. How do they feel about rejection? About the prospect they can't get in to see? About being turned away by the switchboard or shut out by the receptionist. About that day they had a problem with the bank, a problem at home, a problem paying a bill on time, a problem with their spouse, a problem with one of the kids, a problem with the car, a problem with the traffic, a problem with yesterday's clients, a problem getting through to the prospect — and then being flatly put down!

All in the same day. But if your salesperson still has another appointment and a deal to close at 3:30 p.m., that's tenacity!

Understanding

6.   U is for Understanding

Understanding is about listening. A good way to discuss understanding is to ask these questions:

- When did you last listen to a customer?

- What did you hear?

This can lead to some healthy, meaningful dialogue with your team, so be prepared to allow sufficient time.

If you fully understand your prospects, where they are coming from, and what their company's needs are, then you'll be much better positioned to make a sale. But you can't get anywhere unless you focus on listening to your customer — and then on understanding.

You can also approach the word "understanding" this way:

"Well, good morning everyone. I think it's time we had an understanding. Let's talk about it.

We need more business in this company and we need you to dig for it. We're prepared to do everything we can from a production standpoint, a service standpoint, a delivery standpoint, and an administrative standpoint.

Now, *what can you do for us?*"

In the Everest Light Expedition, the team had a definite understanding. While they would all work together to get to the top of that famous mountain, each climber made a commitment to themselves and to the other members of the team and had an understanding of what had to be done to reach the summit.

And at the end of the day, no matter how prepared each of them might have been to attempt those last few feet to the top, the team leader had the final call on who would be chosen for that historic occasion.

Dedication

7. D is for Dedication

I'm not sure as a sales manager you'll be able to teach dedication. I think it's something that happens over a period of time. Just as loyalty and trust are not instant, I believe you and your company and your people together build an environment that allows dedication to happen.

You may certainly discuss with your sales force how they feel individually and collectively about the subject of dedication. Ask these questions:

- Does dedication mean helping the customer?

- Do we mean dedication to the company's mission statement?

- Does it mean dedication to providing a quality product or service to the customer, and if so what controls do your salespeople have in guaranteeing that this happens?

- Does it just mean dedication to the task at hand? Or dedication to the bigger picture? What *is* the bigger picture?

Excellence

8. E is for Excellence

It is fitting that the final word to illustrate the elements in the word Attitude is excellence because it summarizes all of the other words and how they relate to the field of selling.

Again, here is an opportunity for plenty of discussion with your salespeople. Ask these questions:

- Does excellence mean we make the best products?

- Does excellence mean we provide the highest level of services?

- Does excellence mean we're better than everyone else?

c. Setting the Stage for Your Presentation

You can take all this one step further and use the climbing analogy throughout your Attitude Sales Meeting to get everyone cranked up. This is what I have done — and it's always worked well.

If you don't know an avid, gear-equipped climber but have an outdoors shop nearby, borrow or rent some technical climbing equipment. Spend some time with your supplier and understand what the gear is used for (and be prepared to work the various items into your Attitude overheads.)

While I normally pack along a variety of actual Everest expedition souvenirs picked up along the trip through Tibetan villages and from the marketplace in Lhasa, must-pack items include things you can work into your presentation:

- a length of climbing rope (long enough so that when it's uncoiled, everyone in the room can hold onto it at the same time)

- some carabiners (climbers call them "beeners") so that each person can play with and "fix" onto the rope

- a variety of metal pitons, those spike-like gadgets used for driving into cracks as climbing aids or protection

- a climbing harness of nylon webbing

- an ice axe (interesting, serious, deadly looking — a great prop)

- crampons (spiked platforms for attachment to boots for safety on glacial ice or hardpack snow)

Pack all the gear into a large, colorful rucksack and when you arrive at the meeting, have the rucksack ready for tossing onto the table with a dramatic flourish. As you move through your presentation you can then pull from the bag items as you need them, creating plenty of drama along the way.

An important ingredient to the success of this presentation is the high level of interaction between you and everyone else in the room. Get participants to hold onto a piece of the rope and pass some along, then have them "fix" onto the rope, so they can pull it together as a team.

You can modify the Attitude artwork to use for other purposes as well. I've created reduced versions of the mountain climber image and had them laminated to the back of business cards to create an interesting and memorable luggage tag. (See Sample #4). To really add color, you can put your Attitude reminder message in front of your reps on a daily basis by taking the luggage tags and converting them into key holders with a miniature "beener" (it's perfect for snapping open to hold key rings). I've also added a couple of inches of colorful, woven, nylon cord so it looks like a miniature version of the climbing rope used at the meeting.

Remember, though, the comment I made at the beginning of this chapter. *Present all of this with plenty of positive attitude yourself!*

Sample #4
Luggage tags

Part 2
Brilliant Sales Contests

9

The Sales Contest

a. Why Sales Contests?

Question: Why a sales contest?

Answer: To crank 'em up...so they'll sell more!

Ask yourself why you want to run a contest at all:

- To turn a slow selling season into a fast one?
- To move special products/services?
- To create or revive team spirit?
- To break from the daily grind?
- Because the salespeople appear to have lost their aggressive edge?
- Because the competition just hit us where we live?
- To introduce something new? (new prices, new products, etc.)
- To provide a quick sales hit?

One definition of a contest is "a competitive game." And to me a business sales contest is just as simple. It's a special promotion created by a company to generate extra sales-to-budget. It makes the company's cash register ring a whole lot louder. It's a business game.

Sales contests can be created for either internal or external use, but in this book I focus on the internal variety. These are proven promotional techniques that include an element of creativity. They should help you push your sales team just a little harder over the top to sales success.

Added sales garnered through contesting represents billions upon billions of dollars throughout North American business, yet successful contests still use the most basic of ingredients and the simplest of recipes.

When thinking about sales contests you should always consider the following:

(a) Involve as many people in the organization as possible: sales, administration, accounting and finance, manufacturing, distribution, installation, and service. Attempt to create something that cranks up everyone!

(b) Set realistic budgets. It's highly unlikely that a strong and well-promoted contest will double your sales. Be realistic. If you aim for 10% over where you normally would expect to be during a given period, and hit that target or more, you've done well.

(c) Use themes — it's the creative whack! It's the sizzle that sells the steak! Clever, well-thought-out themes are the magic threads that tie so much of your contest together. And it's what makes business fun!

(d) "Incentify" to motivate. Create and spin as many incentives into your contest as possible. Remember, peer pressure within the team works as well as big bucks. Create incentives in such a manner that everyone can be a winner.

Incentives come in many forms. Remember, what motivates and turns up sales productivity with one rep may not crank up another. Some people want to get their hands on quick, weekend cash; others want retail goods, tangible prizes they can use in business or at home to play with, share, and show off. Travel turns the cranks of many — and yes, that thrill of just plain winning, moving ahead of competition can be the number one incentive of all.

(e) Think about timing because timing is everything. Don't go fishing when the fish aren't biting. Be aware of the natural down cycles in sales and adjust your strategies accordingly. And don't miss the boat by running too short a contest because it does take time, especially for larger organizations, to build momentum. Nor should you kill contests by having them drag on. And on. And on.

(f) Communicate results information constantly. This keeps everyone "contest-top-of-mind" and keeps the heat on.

b. Analyzing Your Company's Objectives

Virtually every company initiates promotional schemes of some kind so it is highly unlikely that your company, somewhere in its history, hasn't already involved employees, salespeople, or customers in a contest. They may have worked or they may have bombed, so do a little homework before you launch a new one.

If you're new in your sales management role, it makes good sense to discuss the company's contest history with your salespeople and other departmental managers. Go through as many of the promotions as you can, analyze and critique them, know the ones that worked and why, and the ones that fizzled. During your research, you might already have an idea for a contest and this might be just the right time to test the waters with your concept.

Some themes work a lot better in certain corporate environments than others. If your company has a history of management practices where bosses carried black snake whips, big sticks, and two-by-fours, I doubt that too many of their contests turned sales volumes toward the rafters or motivated the troops to spectacular results. It will be tough to "crank 'em up" unless you know what worked and what didn't.

These days most companies have a mission statement, an established corporate culture, and even a morality that's unique to each company. You should fully understand these areas and discuss them openly with your management colleagues before you start formulating a sales contest. This could save you some in-house, political grief since any theme you develop could run head-on into serious opposition.

Remember, you'll also need budget approvals, and your colleagues in other departments may feel jealous about your dipping into the corporate pot for promotional funds if they have had their own requests for capital expenditures turned down. One of the hardest sales you'll likely have to make is to ask the management committee to expend funds for a colorful sales contest kickoff when they've just announced company-wide budget cuts, staffing layoffs, and the downsizing of their cars!

Since you'll want the full support of the whole management team behind your contest — in fact, you'll want them to turn on everyone in their respective departments too — it's important that you know their feelings and understand their concerns about past contests. Keep in mind that in most instances, non-sales executives and their staff may have never enjoyed participating in a contest of any kind. Part of getting them to buy into yours will be allowing them some "ownership," welcoming their comments up front, and including some of their better thoughts in your game plan.

I've always tried to involve the finance, administration, and production staff in my contest plans, and I've found that they had innovative ideas. They enjoyed participating in kickoffs, the ongoing scoring of the contest results, coaching from the sidelines, and the grand finale conferences.

c. The Targets: Setting Realistic Budgets

Many sales managers I've dealt with would have been quite happy to see any contest at all if it meant the budgets which they had so enthusiastically set for their sales reps earlier in the year were met. You have to wonder if they were realistic in their approach to sales quota budgeting!

Setting budgets at the beginning of the new selling year should involve some careful thinking before target numbers are included. But the task is really quite simple and easily handled. When you're setting preliminary sales budgets, here are some areas to take into consideration:

(a) Overall corporate sales objectives: what the company needs to sell to stay in business

(b) On-the-job experience

(c) Territory (size, opportunity, servicing logistics)

(d) Products/services being sold (regular and new)

(e) Client base (established, new, house accounts)

(f) Remunerative mix (salary, salary plus commission, commission, bonus systems, incentives, and awards)

(g) Education and training

(h) Attitude

(i) Support of company (company attitude toward salespeople)

(j) Personal situations (family, financial, interpersonal skills)

(k) Individual's previous years' sales records

(l) Competitive factors in the marketplace

(m) The economy in general

Be realistic when setting sales targets. If your expectations for each person's quota targets are realistic and therefore doable, then your job of coaching and motivating will be that much more achievable. After all, the way management scores your report card will be heavily weighted toward your ability to achieve the overall numbers you projected at budget time.

d. Setting Sales Contest Quotas

Sales contest quotas must be realistic and achievable. Don't expect to "crank 'em up," and move people to the top of your sales mountain if they can't see the topmost peak.

Don't over-complicate the business of establishing special contest quotas. I've found if the normal sales quotas are realistic, then the contest quotas should be simple to formulate. *Why not just add 5% to 10% to the normal monthly quota set for each person?*

10

Using Contest Themes

As Vice President Marketing, it was my turn to lay out our plans to stay on track during the next quarter.

Reaching under the boardroom table I fumbled around for the masking tape that held the remote control device, activated the power button, and wiggled the toggle switch forward.

Not a word was spoken at the table. The chairman's eyes were glued to the military-style, camouflaged shoe box that I'd plunked down in the center of our quarterly reports, marketing plans, and financial updates.

You could hear a little motor starting up. The shoe box shuddered a bit, one of the end-flaps popped open, and the olive-drab muzzle of a war toy poked out. In seconds a miniature tank, emblazoned with our company's graphics, clattered out of the box, picked up speed over the financial statements, made a sharp right turn, and rumbled on down the boardroom table toward the chairman, Jimmy Pattison.

The rubber tracks easily clamored over operational print-outs, ballpoint pens, handfuls of chewed pencils, and any outstretched palms that dared to remain above the table top. The company flag, fluttering from the radio control antenna, came to an abrupt halt under the skeptical nose of General Patton look-alike Bill Sleeman, the vice-chairman.

I asked Bill to remove one of the two little packages secured to the tank's rear deck, and then let the war machine continue its run toward the head of the table. The tank spun around and stopped smack in the middle of the chairman's notepad. From that vantage point, we all faced the muzzle.

"Jimmy, Bill...your official Claude Army dog tags are right in front of you. Your regimental number on those tags represents the company's total sales objectives for the next quarter — clear targets we've set our gun sights on.

Claude Neon has just declared war on the competition! Times are tough! We're out to win! We have a strategy for a three-month battle plan to capture significant market share on every front! The Great Sign War is under way!" I said.

Fidgeting under the table I stripped off the masking tape and passed the remote controller along to the boss. It was his to kid around with for the rest of the meeting, and later on, to display in his office as a reminder that his sign company was out there fighting for market share.

Now we just had to launch the concept through all our division and branch offices throughout the country and hit our sales targets before the next quarterly meeting!

a. Themes

Contests with themes are easier to package and sell. I can't recall developing or running any sort of a sales contest without first packaging and presenting it with a theme. For contests to have meaning and focus, and to have them stay at the top of the minds of salespeople, and for them to work hard for you, contests must be presented with impact. While theme-packaging your contest doesn't guarantee its ultimate success when the quota tallies are finally in, it certainly allows you to build the contest in many directions using a common promotional thread.

Let's say you were looking to crank up sales over the next few months. Even the simplest of ideas like "top salesperson this month wins a dinner for two at The Cattleman's Steak House" can be presented colorfully.

Obviously the themes you select must fit various criteria factors. A contest that might be very appealing to the men on your sales force for instance, might not enjoy equal success with female reps, or those from a variety of cultural or religious backgrounds. While your personal interests might seem ideal for building a contest theme, you must consider its interest and subsequent impact on the whole sales force.

Go through Checklist #2 whenever you are considering an idea for a theme.

b. Where to Get Great Ideas

Ideas come from everywhere imaginable. My favorite place for finding basic contest concepts and getting the creative kick start I need for brainstorming is a retail store. Not only can you see a tremendous variety of items that will trigger your thoughts, but you can also spot a lot of the collateral materials that you need to embellish your theme.

Checklist #2
Contest Theme Checklist

Use this checklist to review any theme idea you might have.

1. Are there special products you wish to promote? ____

2. Does the selling season fit? ____

3. Are company politics or touchy areas affected? ____

4. Can both men and women get equally enthused? ____

5. What is the length of the contest period? ____

6. Can the budgets handle all facets of the contest? ____

7. Is everything in good taste? ____

8. Does the theme promote ease of handling and logistics? ____

9. Can your non-selling people get involved? ____

10. Can salespeople's families get involved? ____

11. Is there customer involvement? ____

12. Does it suit your sales targets? ____

13. If it is held in multiple locations, can you keep the spirit alive? ____

14. What can you do for the kickoff? ____

15. Can you use communications devices
    like contest releases?   ____

16. Are there promotional giveaway items?   ____

17. Will special, mid-term prizes
    be introduced?   ____

18. How will contest results be announced?   ____

19. What will the contest finale event be?   ____

20. How will prizes be awarded?   ____

Here is a list of retailers that will get your creative juices going:

- Toys
- Games
- Hobbies
- Crafts
- Sporting goods
- Military surplus
- Clearance discount centers
- Antiques and collectibles
- Hardware and home centers
- Clothing
- Outdoor adventure/camping
- Books
- Western
- Auto supply
- Pet
- Department
- Five and dime
- Magic

And here are a few other idea sources:

- Catalogues (all kinds)
- Clip-art reference books
- Print advertising
- Newspapers (dailies, weeklies, business)
- Magazines and periodicals (special interest, general interest)

c. Getting Everyone Involved

While you might create a terrific contest to turn up sales heat within your own department, you should also consider what happens during contest time elsewhere in your organization. My experience has been that the more people in a company who get cranked up, the better the final results.

Whenever I presented the conceptual thinking behind a soon-to-be-launched contest to management, I kept in mind that my audience was made up of executives from many departments *other* than sales and marketing. I included as many of them as I could since I genuinely needed their advice in the early structuring stages.

Invariably, once they listened through a first draft outline, they had plenty of suggestions to help with the operational logistics of the scheme, and of course once our contest was underway, I expected their departmental people to be particularly cooperative and supportive during the heat of the contest.

I knew for instance that additional sales activities meant increased pressure in every department. Our design team would be pushed to move more sketches off their drawing boards, estimators would not have the luxury of extra time with sales reps breathing down their necks for quick quotes to meet contest deadlines, and our credit staff would be pressured to collect and deliver their evaluations in much shorter order than usual.

Since our industry-leading customer service area was one we would never tinker with, it was essential that everyone who dealt with our customers (during contests we worked very hard to increase their business with us), our new clients, and our prospective ones *completely buy into our contest plans*.

Here are a few ideas that might help you maximize behind-the-scenes involvement:

- Hold kickoffs at the workplace (in the office, in the plant, in the parking lot)
- If themes are involved, costumed extras add extra atmosphere and involve willing staff
- Create situations where staff can bet on salespeople: when reps hit targets, the bet pays off (staff keep up the daily pressure)
- Put sales reps and groups of support staff on teams together (staff can support and keep the pressure turned up for even more business)
- Organize prizes that tie into the theme and create opportunities for the behind-the-scenes people to win often
- Decorate the office/plant with themed material. Create a special pizzazz that works for everyone and builds morale
- Publish a contest newsletter or release and circulate widely to everyone in the organization. Mention non-winners too
- Post contest targets on bulletin boards and update with current events

The more people you crank up behind the scenes, the more they crank up your sales team.

d. Using the Theme Concepts and Matrixes

On the following pages, I've supplied a number of mind map theme outlines with accompanying matrixes which you can adapt for your own use. One of the better management techniques I've fine-tuned over the years has been "mind mapping." This technique allows you to quickly create and format an overall picture of a situation or project on just one sheet of a flip chart (or notebook page, white board panel, or computer screen).

I usually combine brainstorming with mind mapping. With a basic "main idea," I can quickly spin off secondary categories and follow them with as many sub-categories as I need.

The following matrixes are idea- and thought-starters. By using a matrix, you can quickly see all the parts needed when structuring a sales contest. The mind map matrixes offer complete contest-at-a-glance planning simplicity, while the outlines provide brief conceptual notes to help move the themes along. If, for instance, you choose sports, feel free to make changes in order to adapt it to the sport you choose.

The last matrix is generic and illustrates most of the key areas worthy of consideration prior to the launching of any contest, regardless of its size or complexity. A blank version follows all the examples, ready for you to fill in. Feel free to copy and enlarge the generic mind map matrix and use it to guide you through the structuring of your own contest requirements.

After using this system a couple of times, you'll find it one of the most convenient planning tools around. Once you've completed a contest mind map, convert it to an overhead acetate and you'll be primed for your presentation to the management group.

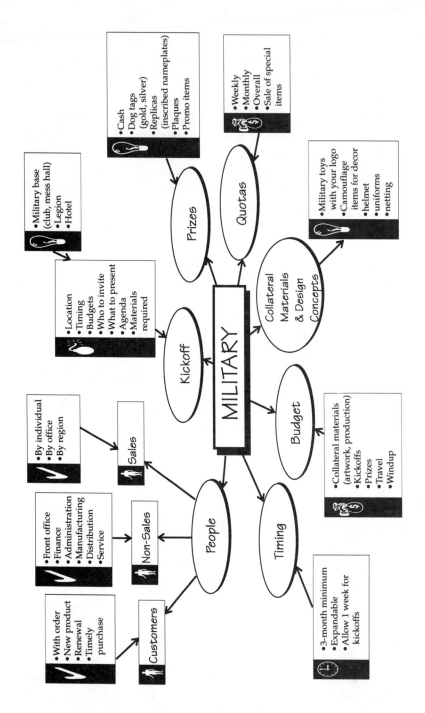

MILITARY

Prizes
- Cash
- Dog tags (gold, silver)
- Replicas (inscribed nameplates)
- Plaques
- Promo items

Quotas
- Weekly
- Monthly
- Overall
- Sale of special items

Collateral Materials & Design Concepts
- Military toys with your logo
- Camouflage items for decor
  - helmet
  - uniforms
  - netting

Kickoff
- Location
- Timing
- Budgets
- Who to invite
- What to present
- Agenda
- Materials required

(Military base (club, mess hall) • Legion • Hotel)

Budget
- Collateral materials (artwork, production)
- Kickoffs
- Prizes
- Travel
- Windup

People

Sales
- By individual
- By office
- By region

Non-Sales
- Front office
- Finance
- Administration
- Manufacturing
- Distribution
- Service

Customers
- With order
- New product
- Renewal
- Timely purchase

Timing
- 3-month minimum
- Expandable
- Allow 1 week for kickoffs

Theme: Military
(Army, Navy, Air Force, Marines, Coast Guard)

Rationale:

- groups and individuals can compete
- clients can be tied in
- will work better over three-month period than less
- everyone behind scenes can become involved
- aggressively exciting, colorful
- easy to relate to

Creative concepts:

- at war with the competition
- at war with prices
- company becomes one of the military branches
- regional offices become posts, squadrons, wings, ships, regiments, or platoons — whatever fits the branch structure
- corporate offices become headquarters (HQ), war offices, bunkers, or command posts
- management has ranks from CEO through to sales reps
- can be kicked off in "camouflaged, secret war room" or possibly at an actual military base, ship, legion hall, etc.
- scoring is based on sales made, quotas scored, battles won, victories achieved, market share
- military theme at each location
- props etc. not costly and easily obtainable
- prizes: plaques, gold or silver dog tags, miniature guns, aircraft, boats suitably mounted with engraved plaques, cash, special commission structures

Material sources:

- surplus stores, libraries, toy stores

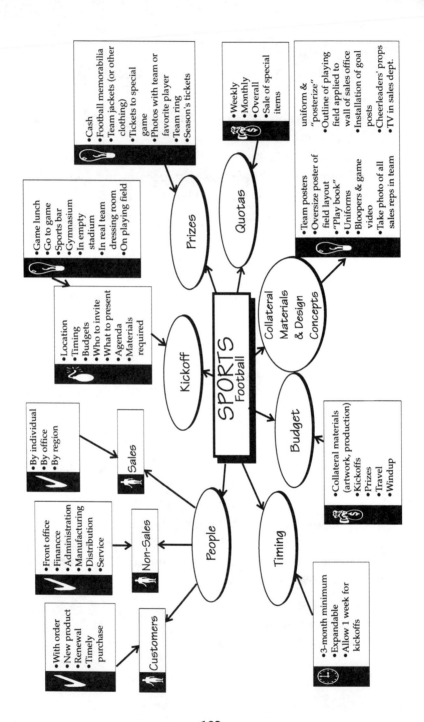

SPORTS Football

Prizes
- Cash
- Football memorabilia
- Team jackets (or other clothing)
- Tickets to special game
- Photos with team or favorite player
- Team ring
- Season's tickets

Quotas
- Weekly
- Monthly
- Overall
- Sale of special items

Collateral Materials & Design Concepts
- Team posters
- Oversize poster of field layout
- "Play book"
- Uniforms
- Bloopers & game video
- Take photo of all sales reps in team
- uniform & "posterize"
- Outline of playing field applied to wall of sales office
- Installation of goal posts
- Cheerleaders' props
- TV in sales dept.

Kickoff
- Location
- Timing
- Budgets
- Who to invite
- What to present
- Agenda
- Materials required
- Game lunch
- Go to game
- Sports bar
- Gymnasium
- In empty stadium
- In real team dressing room
- On playing field

Sales
- By individual
- By office
- By region

Non-Sales
- Front office
- Finance
- Administration
- Manufacturing
- Distribution
- Service

Customers
- With order
- New product
- Renewal
- Timely purchase

People

Budget
- Collateral materials (artwork, production)
- Kickoffs
- Prizes
- Travel
- Windup

Timing
- 3-month minimum
- Expandable
- Allow 1 week for kickoffs

Theme: Sports — Football

Rationale:

- groups and individuals can compete
- clients can be tied in
- works well over last three months of actual football season, as your playoffs (call them payoffs) can coincide
- can involve whole company
- highly competitive in nature
- inexpensive to create atmosphere/theme
- easy to keep up the pressure

Creative concepts:

- offices can compete with each other
- regions can play off against each other
- individuals can go for yardage
- each office adopts name of real team or creates their own
- salespeople are the players; sales managers the coaches, and sales offices the bench, team room, or locker room
- kickoffs can take place at high school, college, or university football field, professional stadium or locker rooms; or set up a meeting room as locker room, or reserve a sports bar; have a game lunch; use gymnasium
- end of contest event at one of above
- prizes: cash, football memorabilia, team jackets, sweatshirts, special game tickets, team photos, team rings, season's tickets to next year's games

Material sources:

- sporting goods stores, toy stores, football league marketing offices, national league football team marketing office, colleges, universities, high school teams

Theme: Sports — Baseball

Rationale:

- groups and individuals can compete
- clients can be tied in
- works well over a shortened baseball season (three-month period ideal)
- can involve everyone behind scenes
- highly competitive in nature
- colorful
- inexpensive to create atmosphere/theme
- easy to keep at the top of everyone's mind

Creative concepts:

- offices compete with each other
- regions can play off against each other for "World Series"
- each office adopts name of real team or creates fictitious name (e.g., Barney's Bears)
- salespeople are the players; sales managers are the coaches; sales offices are the dugouts
- kickoffs can take place outdoors at a baseball diamond, stadium, real locker room, or locker room setup
- props can include hats, jackets, bats, balls, gloves, bases, spikes, team uniforms, sweatshirts, t-shirts
- prizes: team jackets, autographed balls, sweatshirts, game tickets, trips to World Series, joining a baseball spring training adult guest camp, cash, special commission structures

Material sources:

- sporting goods stores, toy stores, baseball league marketing offices, major league baseball team marketing offices

Theme: Sports — Basketball

Rationale:

- groups and individuals can compete; clients can be tied in; can involve everyone in company
- works well over a shortened basketball season; three-month period ideal
- highly competitive in nature; easy to keep pressure on
- colorful; inexpensive to create atmosphere/theme

Creative concepts:

- offices can compete with each other; regions can play off
- each office adopts name of a real team or creates fictitious name
- office decorations: team pennants, posters, uniforms, photos, miniature baskets over garbage cans, larger baskets in staff room, sales office, etc.
- salespeople are the players; sales are baskets; sales managers the coaches; sales offices the benches, etc.
- kickoffs and grand finales can be staged at gymnasiums, team tables (dinners), sports bars, actual locker rooms or locker room setups
- prizes: team jackets, sweatshirts, game tickets, photos with team, trips to championships, cash, special commission structures, season's tickets for next year

Material sources:

- sporting goods stores, toy stores, basketball league marketing offices, professional basketball team marketing offices, high schools, colleges, universities

Note: You can adapt this matrix to include other sports themes like golf, sailing, hockey, etc.

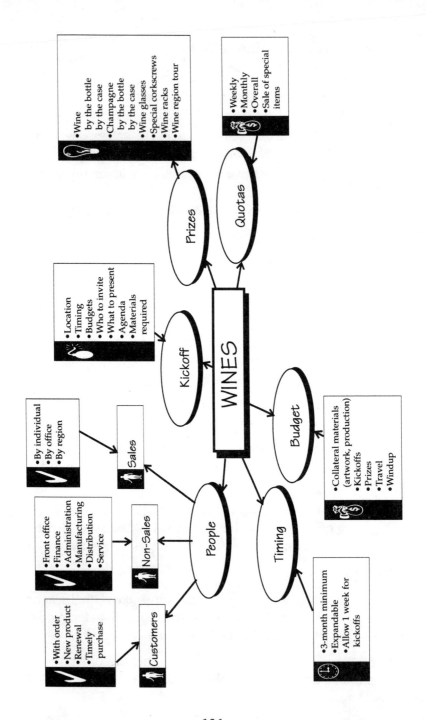

WINES

Prizes
- Wine
  by the bottle
  by the case
- Champagne
  by the bottle
  by the case
- Wine glasses
- Special corkscrews
- Wine racks
- Wine region tour

Quotas
- Weekly
- Monthly
- Overall
- Sale of special items

Kickoff
- Location
- Timing
- Budgets
- Who to invite
- What to present
- Agenda
- Materials required

Sales
- By individual
- By office
- By region

Non-Sales
- Front office
- Finance
- Administration
- Manufacturing
- Distribution
- Service

Customers
- With order
- New product
- Renewal
- Timely purchase

People

Budget
- Collateral materials (artwork, production)
- Kickoffs
- Prizes
- Travel
- Windup

Timing
- 3-month minimum
- Expandable
- Allow 1 week for kickoffs

Theme: Wines

Rationale:

- groups and individuals can compete; clients can be tied-in; works well over a three-month period
- everyone behind scenes can become involved and win a prize of some kind
- colorful; inexpensive to create atmosphere/theme; easy to understand; any time is good
- each person can set own pace and better it

Concept:

- create a wine-growing region; head office is "Chateau (add co. name)"
- offices can become cellars, with managers becoming sommeliers (keepers of wine cellars); sales reps become "growers" (and "grow" more business)
- regions can become vineyards (you could describe the sales activities of a given region during a contest by saying, "Growers from the ABC Cellars of Chateau XYZ's vineyards have reported in with a bountiful harvest of new contracts...")
- decorations at offices can include posters, displays with wine racks, bottles of wine/champagne, and related props
- scoring is based on sales to quota either individually or as a team
- can be kicked off at wine tastings by knowledgeable wine industry reps; special wine appreciation dinner for winners; other prizes: wines (single bottles, cases), champagnes, wine glasses, special openers/corkscrews with logo, wine racks, tour of wine regions

Material sources:

- food and wine section of libraries, wine importers, fine restaurants, liquor/wine retailers, wine growers, library, wine hobbyist retailers

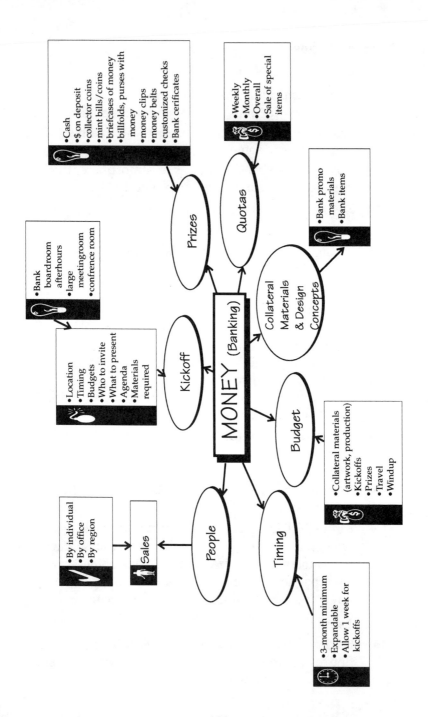

Theme — Money — Banking

Rationale:
- groups and individuals can compete; works well over a three-month period
- colorful; inexpensive to create atmosphere/theme

Creative concepts:
- company becomes a Bank (ACME Manufacturing becomes Bank of ACME)
- top management become bankers, sales management becomes tellers, sales reps become depositors (and deposit new business to the company) since business equals dollars, and dollars get deposited
- prior to contest kickoff, create and open fictitious account for each sales rep (and his or her spouse) and show "on deposit" a given amount of funds
- each time sales rep hits a specific target, additional funds or credits are deposited in the account. If targets are not hit, "withdrawals" are made
- at kickoff, set up "teller's cage" with a sales manager behind it. Give each sales rep a bank book showing the funds "on deposit." Include rules and what products/services mean in deposit amounts
- winners should win actual joint accounts with funds they earn on deposit
- prizes can include cash, dollars on deposit, mint coins/bills, etc.

Material sources:
- bank promotional materials, various bank items (checks, etc.), libraries, financial reference libraries

Note: You can adapt this matrix to other money themes like the stock market, gambling, lotteries, and cash.

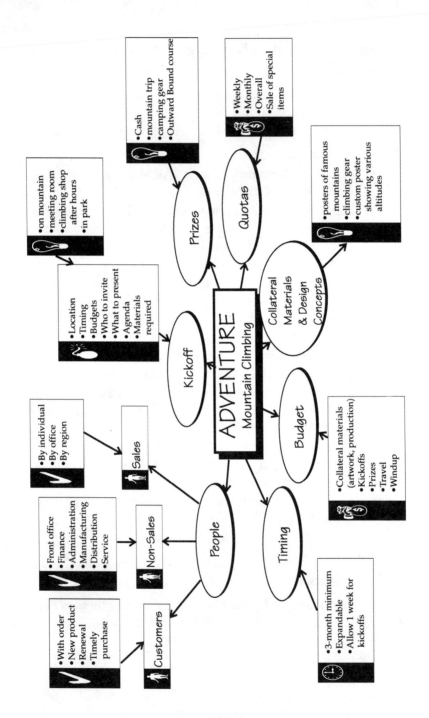

ADVENTURE
Mountain Climbing

Prizes
• Cash
• mountain trip
• camping gear
• Outward Bound course

Quotas
• Weekly
• Monthly
• Overall
• Sale of special items

Collateral Materials & Design Concepts
• posters of famous mountains
• climbing gear
• custom poster showing various altitudes

Kickoff
• Location
• Timing
• Budgets
• Who to invite
• What to present
• Agenda
• Materials required

on mountain
• meeting room
• climbing shop after hours
• in park

Sales
• By individual
• By office
• By region

People

Non-Sales
• Front office
• Finance
• Administration
• Manufacturing
• Distribution
• Service

Customers
• With order
• New product
• Renewal
• Timely purchase

Budget
• Collateral materials (artwork, production)
• Kickoffs
• Prizes
• Travel
• Windup

Timing
• 3-month minimum
• Expandable
• Allow 1 week for kickoffs

Theme: Adventure — Mountain Climbing

Rationale:
- groups and individuals can compete
- clients can be tied-in
- works well over a three-month period
- can involve everyone behind scenes
- highly competitive in nature
- colorful
- inexpensive to create atmosphere/theme
- each person can set own pace and better it

Creative concepts:
- top of the mountain can be:
    target of whole company
    target of branch or regional office
    target of individual
- create silhouette artwork of mountain and mark various "altitude levels," or sales targets from bottom to top. If over a three-month period, you might create monthly "altitides" that must be obtained. When these are totalled they would reach the peak (the sales summit!)
- salespeople are the climbers, with sales managers becoming team leaders
- use climbing apparatus to decorate sales and front offices
- kickoffs can take place outdoors at or near a mountainous area, or some cities have sports facilities that offer indoor climbing outfits. You can take a team to a specially equipped facility after hours and everyone can learn to climb the walls using devices attached to

the inner walls. Proper gear, training, and complete safety are usually highlighted attractions

- all salespeople can be on the same rope during kickoff
- you might also wish to contact a wilderness or adventure school organization to help you create the atmosphere
- invite famous mountaineers to give motivational talks and relate their adventures and accomplishments
- props can include climbing gear, real climbing ropes, pitons, crampons, helmets, beeners, climbing harnesses, rucksacks, posters, outdoor clothing
- create an oversize picture or model of a mountain for display in your sales office or meeting room (for the kickoff). Show levels of achievement ($x = x feet/meters); put them up on the mountain.
- sales of various products/services etc. can move sales reps up the mountain (some products are worth more altitude than others)
- prizes: cash and adventure trips (the Outward Bound organization has adventure school locations around the world) are easy to arrange for one or more winners. And your people come back with a very special "I can do it" attitude that will keep them high on the sales charts.

Material sources:
- outdoor/adventure retailers
- sporting goods stores
- library for climbing books
- outdoor/climbing clubs and associations

- travel agents (Himalayas/Rockies/Andes/Alps, etc.)
- posters of famous mountains and/or mountaineers

Note: You can adapt this matrix to include other adventure themes, like westerns, gold rushes, safaris, outer space wars, and pirate treasure hunts, etc.

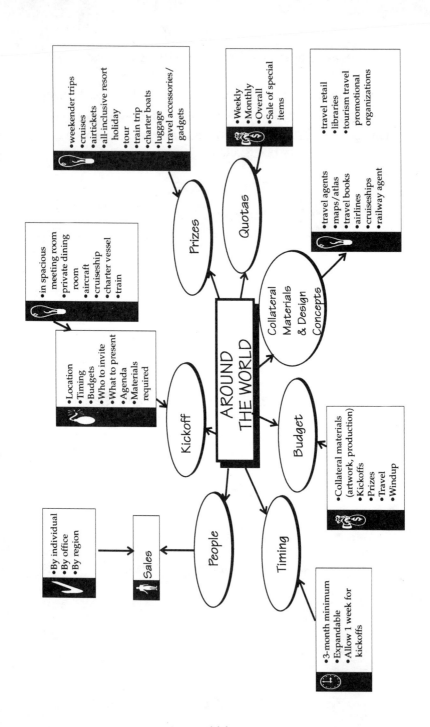

AROUND THE WORLD

Prizes
- weekender trips
- cruises
- airtickets
- all-inclusive resort holiday
- tour
- train trip
- charter boats
- luggage
- travel accessories/gadgets

Quotas
- Weekly
- Monthly
- Overall
- Sale of special items

Kickoff
- Location
- Timing
- Budgets
- Who to invite
- What to present
- Agenda
- Materials required

Kickoff location:
- in spacious meeting room
- private dining room
- aircraft
- cruiseship
- charter vessel
- train

Collateral Materials & Design Concepts
- travel agents
- maps/atlas
- travel books
- airlines
- cruiseships
- railway agent
- travel retail
- libraries
- tourism travel promotional organizations

Budget
- Collateral materials (artwork, production)
- Kickoffs
- Prizes
- Travel
- Windup

People
- By individual
- By office
- By region

Sales

Timing
- 3-month minimum
- Expandable
- Allow 1 week for kickoffs

Theme — Travel — Around the World

Rationale:

- individuals can compete; works well over a three-month period
- extremely colorful; inexpensive to create atmosphere/theme; behind scenes staff can participate

Creative concepts:

- points (based on dollar value or volume of goods/services sold-to-quota) are awarded. These points translate to mileage. Mileage accumulated gets participants where they want to go or gets a specific prize of that value
- use maps, atlas, pictures/drawings of locations around the world
- number of prizes could total 80, ranging in items as small and inexpensive as postcards to luggage to weekend trips to luxurious extended period trips to all-inclusive resorts
- kickoffs could include a "taste of the world" with booths, each serving a taste from the far corners of the world. These should be set up in a large meeting room for a "world market" atmosphere. Kickoffs could also take place inside a mockup aircraft where actual airline food is served by staff and announcements are made regarding the sales contest rules or on a train or a charter boat.

Material sources:

- travel agencies, maps/atlas/guidebooks, tourism promotional organizations, airlines/cruise ship companies or charter boat/bus lines, retail stores catering to travelers (luggage)

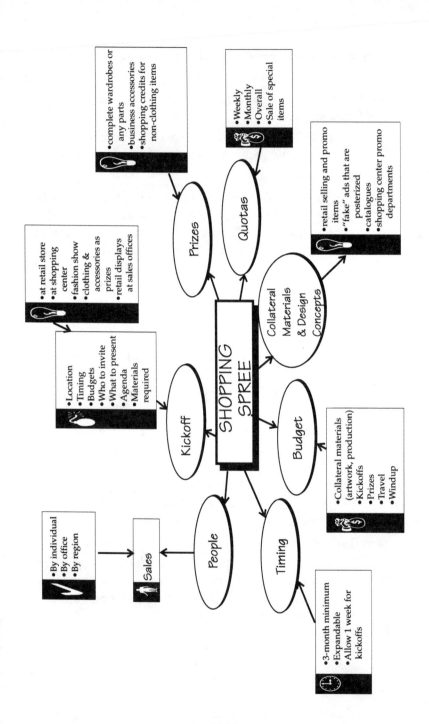

SHOPPING SPREE

Prizes
- complete wardrobes or any parts
- business accessories
- shopping credits for non-clothing items

Quotas
- Weekly
- Monthly
- Overall
- Sale of special items

Collateral Materials & Design Concepts
- retail selling and promo items
- "fake" ads that are posterized
- catalogues
- shopping center promo departments

Kickoff
- at retail store
- at shopping center
- fashion show
- clothing & accessories as prizes
- retail displays at sales offices

- Location
- Timing
- Budgets
- Who to invite
- What to present
- Agenda
- Materials required

Budget
- Collateral materials (artwork, production)
- Kickoffs
- Prizes
- Travel
- Windup

People

Timing
- 3-month minimum
- Expandable
- Allow 1 week for kickoffs

Sales
- By individual
- By office
- By region

Theme — Retail — Shopping Spree

Rationale:

- individuals can compete
- works well over a two- or three-month period before Christmas
- colorful
- inexpensive to create atmosphere/theme
- each person can set own pace and better it

Creative concepts:

- arrange with well-known retailer(s) to provide complete wardrobes for winners (male/female) from shoes to overcoats
- hold kickoff at retail store after hours and stage special sales fashion show (if possible, invite non-sales people to be the models)
- base contest on percentage-to-quota and create a point structure in which points are worth credits toward the wardrobe or parts of it
- displays in sales departments could be similar to product or window displays at the retailers you are working with
- decorative items, sale banners, and other retail display items can be rented or borrowed from the retailers or manufacturers of the clothing
- arrange contest so winners are rewarded before Christmas

Material sources:

- Retailers
- Clothing designers/manufacturers/sales agencies
- Shopping center promo departments

Note: You can adapt this matrix to include other retail themes like clothing, electronics, and appliances.

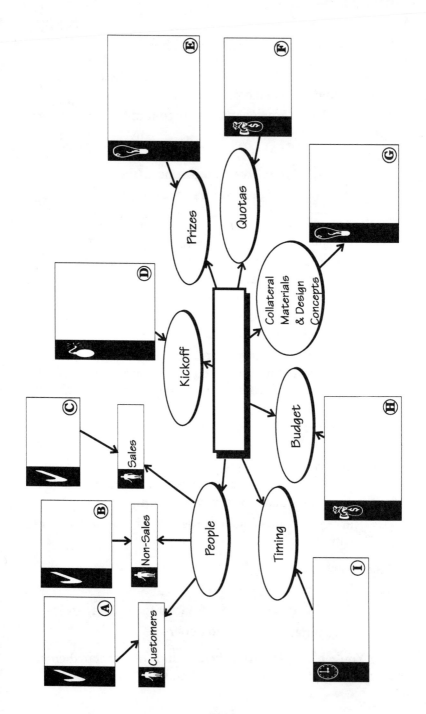

e. Make Your Own Theme Concept and Matrix

Now that you have seen how the sample matrixes can be used to organize ideas around the theme, try jotting down your own ideas. If you've got a theme in mind, jot down ideas for the following:

- How can your customers can get involved?

_____
_____
_____
_____

- Who could participate behind the scenes?

_____
_____
_____
_____

- How does your department compete?

_____
_____
_____
_____

- List all kickoff details.

_____
_____
_____
_____

- List ideas that will make your kickoff unique

_____
_____
_____
_____

This is the place to list all the ideas you have about prizes. Include the zaniest, the cheapest, the most expensive, but tie them into your theme.

Decide how you will structure quotas and what dollar volume they should represent to your overall budget.

Consider the time it takes to set up a contest, hold kickoffs in more than one location, keep interest high, properly monitor results, and close down.

Get Some Feedback
On Your Contest

I like to find out about what's worked for others and I constantly look for ideas and thought-starters. I go through every section of three or four newspapers in the morning and clip and file notes and articles for inspiration. Hopefully, you've picked up some ideas to add to your own folder. Maybe you can now create the contest of the decade and make it sing.

I'd be pleased to hear all about your contesting efforts. Take a moment to collect your thoughts, opinions, and comments. Feel free to include any information you wish. Then package up whatever you want to share with me (see next page).

As time permits, I'll personally review your contest information and *informally* critique it for you. Please note that I am unable to return your materials and that by forwarding them to me you are agreeing that we have your and your company's permission to use the material in subsequent books that may be published or in presentations I might make.

Be sure to enclose a self-addressed, stamped envelope and forward to:

Bruce Fuller
President, The Pacific Partners Communications Group
Suite 1401 - 1166 Alberni Street
Vancouver, B.C.
Canada   V6E 3Z3

Contest Critique

Please provide the following information:

Your name_____
(also enclose your business card)

Company_____

Address_____

City_____State/Province_____

Country_____ Zip/Postal Code_____

Telephone (   )_____ Fax (   )_____

Contest name_____

Describe:

Basic theme/concept_____

Contest rules_____
_____
_____
_____

How quotas were structured_____
_____
_____
_____

Prizes/rewards/incentives_____
_____
_____
_____

Timing_____
_____

Who got involved?
　　　　Sales?_____ Customers?_____ Non-sales_____

What collateral materials were developed? (send photos, etc. if possible)

_____

_____

_____

_____

Sources for collateral material_____

_____

_____

Kickoffs: Where? When? Unique (how)?_____

_____

_____

_____

_____

Budgets: How did you structure them? Were you over? Under? On target?_____

_____

_____

_____

_____

What made this contest special?_____

_____

_____

_____

_____

Results: Did your contest achieve its objectives? What were the objectives?_____

_____

_____

_____

_____

If you have enjoyed this book and would like to receive a free catalogue of all Self-Counsel titles, please write to the appropriate address below:

Self-Counsel Press
1481 Charlotte Road
North Vancouver, B.C.
V7J 1H1

Self-Counsel Press
1704 N. State Street
Bellingham, Washington
98225